Jews and Christians in Dialogue:

New Testament Foundations

Jews and Christians in Dialogue

NEW TESTAMENT FOUNDATIONS

by
JOHN KOENIG

THE WESTMINSTER PRESS
Philadelphia

BOOK DESIGN BY DOROTHY ALDEN SMITH

First edition

Published by The Westminster Press®
Philadelphia, Pennsylvania

PRINTED IN THE UNITED STATES OF AMERICA
9 8 7 6 5 4 3 2 1

Library of Congress Cataloging in Publication Data

Koenig, John, 1938–
Jews and Christians in dialogue.

Bibliography: p.
Includes index.
1. Jews in the New Testament. 2. Bible. N.T.—
Criticism, interpretation, etc. I. Title.
BS2545.J44K63   225.6   79–17583
ISBN 0–664–24280–4

For my parents,
who taught me to honor
the sons and daughters
of Israel

CONTENTS

New Testament Foundations for Jewish-Christian Dialogue

I have written this book as a Christian to Christians; but I send it on its way in the hope that our Jewish brothers and sisters will be reading it over our shoulders, or better yet, at our sides. Today, from whatever perspective we join the dialogue, we need to keep one another informed about what we are telling our own constituencies. For Christians, such a process must always include a kind of public wrestling match with those most treasured documents of our faith called the New Testament. I trust that in the pages that follow, this wrestling will become evident to all readers.

The Anti-Defamation League of B'nai B'rith in New York receives a number of communications each year from concerned Jews who feel that they have encountered anti-Semitic attitudes, words, or acts. What may surprise many Christians is that in recent years some of these complaints have centered on the New Testament. It is not unusual that a traveler who chances upon a Gideon Bible in a motel room pages through the Gospels or Paul's letters for the first time. Certain passages seem definitely hostile toward Jews and Judaism.[1] One must of course inquire about the details of the various incidents in order to evaluate them fairly, but the sad fact remains that for a variety of reasons some Jews do indeed experience the New Testament as anti-Semitic literature.

An unusual variation on this theme appears in a letter from an Eastern European Christian of Jewish origin to the editors of *Christi-*

anity Today. Mr. Rachmiel Frydland Rov's response is to an editorial in the magazine which had, among other things, denied charges that the New Testament contains distorted pictures of Jews and Judaism.[2] The closing words of Mr. Rov's letter reveal his own mixed feelings on the matter:

> I have been now an evangelical believer for forty years. In pre-World War II days, some German evangelicals were invited to preach alternately in the Jewish mission house (since the German language is so like the Yiddish that we spoke). Invariably two of these evangelicals would often choose a text from John, especially 8:44, to show us Jews our sinfulness. In both cases, when Hitler invaded Poland, they became the most ardent Hitler supporters, and their sons joined the S.S., which performed the Jewish exterminations. The ones . . . who risked their lives to preserve us somehow left out these verses when they preached at us and never threw them in our faces. I realize this is an argument of *post hoc ergo propter hoc,* logically invalid, yet for the sake of the Gospel among Israel it is worthwhile to consider.[3]

The passage cited from John, which is unique to the Fourth Gospel, shows Jesus denouncing some of his Jewish opponents as follows: "You are of your father the devil, and your will is to do your father's desires. He was a murderer from the beginning, and has nothing to do with the truth." We shall deal with the obvious hostility reflected here in Chapter 6.

Whether or not the New Testament actually contains anti-Semitic statements, the message of Mr. Rov's poignant letter seems to be that certain passages can be effectively claimed and exploited by those who are inclined to despise Jews—with terrifying results. On the other hand, Christians who feel positively toward Jews will tend to "edit out" those parts of the New Testament which seem to condemn them for rejecting and/or killing Jesus. According to Mr. Rov, the question of how the New Testament operates as a causal factor in creating such radically different postures toward Jews will probably remain unanswered.

Perhaps. But two recent scholarly treatments of the New Testament take up the issue seriously. In her book *Faith and Fratricide: The Theological Roots of Anti-Semitism,* Christian theologian Rosemary Ruether argues that many sections of the New Testament were *intended* by their authors to foster hostile attitudes toward Jews. As Professor Ruether sees it, the very naming of Jesus as Christ initiates a type of anti-Judaism, i.e., a rejection or dismissal of Jews who do not accept Jesus' Messiahship, along with a condescending attitude toward the Jewish religion.[4]

Dr. Samuel Sandmel, formerly of Cincinnati's Hebrew Union College and now Helen A. Regenstein Professor of Religion at the University of Chicago, has proved himself an empathetic conversation partner with Christians over the years.[5] However, in one of his latest books, *Anti-Semitism in the New Testament?* he feels bound to conclude that the New Testament does indeed contain much that should be labeled anti-Semitic.[6] To make his point, Professor Sandmel works through the New Testament book by book, endeavoring to show where its authors have purposely sketched Jews or Judaism in an unfavorable light. The examples he cites are legion.

In the face of this impressive evidence, we Christians may feel overwhelmed by anger or defensiveness about our New Testament Scriptures. (We tend to feel such charges couldn't be true.) Conversely, we may experience embarrassment and guilt over the books that have nurtured our faith, or feel disillusioned about their authority for our lives today. I for one do not believe that we need to suffer the extremes of wounded pride or gloom in this matter. Nor do we need nervously to set aside our New Testaments when participating in Jewish-Christian dialogue. Rather, what we need is to read our earliest Christian sources more carefully.

Although I have profited a great deal from the insights of Professors Ruether and Sandmel, I think they do not wrestle long enough with the complexities of the first Christian documents. Most of the prominent New Testament authors were Jews who continued to affirm their Jewishness even as they wrote about Jesus.[7] Thus it seems necessary, from a historical point of view, to treat them as "Jewish Christians" and to explore the full ambiguity of that title.

Much has happened recently in the scholarly study of the first century to help us in our search. In fact, it is my conviction that with the aid of contemporary Biblical scholarship we Christians can come to see in our New Testament a band of witnesses which, on the whole, proves far more pro-Jewish and pro-Judaistic than we imagine. Our New Testament writers exhibit a curious ambivalence about their mother religion. This results in contradictory statements about the continuing value of Judaism for Christians (see, e.g., Mt. 23:1–2) and leaves us with the impression that while Jewish-Christian relations are addressed in the New Testament, they are never really "settled."

I believe that this very lack of finality can work to benefit Jewish-Christian dialogue in our day. We Christians will continue to regard the New Testament as authoritative when it speaks with clarity and unanimity. When it does not, we shall want to open ourselves to the guidance of the Holy Spirit. God has not yet finished his "new creation" (see 2 Cor. 5:17, which is based on Is. 43:18–21; 65:17ff.)[8] In all probability, this ongoing redemption holds many surprises for us—as it obviously did for the apostle Paul (2 Cor. 1:8–11). At the very least, God's unfolding plan calls us to a constantly renewed mind about our New Testament sources. This will include a heightened sensitivity both to the undeniably hostile passages in our Scriptures and to those more numerous places which manifest a profound sympathy toward Jews and Judaism.

The memory of the Holocaust may play a role here. Perhaps as a result of the recent prominence given to this most tragic and inexplicable of modern events, a great many Christian people, from all walks of life, are entering into conversations with their Jewish neighbors. What I hope to show in the following chapters is that the New Testament offers Jew and Christian alike more resources for this emerging dialogue than obstacles to it, especially at the grass-roots level.

Prior to the more technical work of exegesis, however, we need to clarify some terms that will appear throughout the book:

1. I have already called attention to the phrase "Jewish Christian." I believe this category to be historically defensible, and I shall apply it regularly both to the Jewish authors of the New Testament and to the first Christian church in Jerusalem. Today, when referring to Jews who have adopted Christianity, we should probably speak about

"Christians of Jewish origin"; for the debate over whether one can any longer claim both a Jewish and a Christian identity is far from resolved.

2. In dealing with what we Christians call the "Old Testament," I shall use the term "Hebrew Scriptures" or, in the case of their earliest translation into Greek, the "Septuagint" (abbreviated LXX). Some Jewish scholars feel comfortable talking about the Old Testament, inasmuch as they understand "Old" to mean "ancient" rather than "outmoded." Nevertheless, because this Christian title can lead us to presume that the Hebrew part of our Bible has been superseded by the New Testament, I shall avoid it in the pages that follow.

3. One of the words occurring most frequently in the New Testament is "Israel." By my count, there are sixty-seven distinct references. As far as I can tell, not one of these describes the Christian church (as in the unfortunate and non-Biblical expression "new Israel"), or even those ethnic Jews who believe in Jesus' Messiahship. Instead, the term everywhere denotes empirical Israel, that is, the Jewish nation that once covenanted with God at Sinai and/or its physical heirs in first-century Judaism.[9] At certain points this predominant meaning is supplemented, though not replaced, by an eschatological one. In such cases, we might translate our word "Israel as it will become at the end of time" (see Mt. 19:28; Lk. 22:30; Rom. 11:26). The point here is that while no New Testament writer wished to give up continuity with the original people of God, neither did any of them make that continuity into a simple equation between Israel and church.[10]

4. Finally, after considerable thought, I have decided to employ the term "anti-Judaism" for those statements in the New Testament which reflect antagonism toward Jews and their religion. One reason for preferring this phrase over "anti-Semitism" is that most of the hostile words we shall encounter in our investigation of the New Testament issue from people who were themselves Jews. We have something of an analogy in the Qumran covenanters. Although these first-century Jews practically wrote off the official Judaism of their day, they are not generally classified as anti-Semitic by modern scholars. Similar restraint should probably be applied to historical treat-

ments of first-century Jewish Christians, at least to those who lived and wrote before the official split between church and synagogue (see Chapter 3). A second reason for using "anti-Judaism" instead of "anti-Semitism" is that the latter term has acquired such a massive and hateful baggage in the course of our two-thousand-year Jewish-Christian history. It seems unfair to impute all of this to the New Testament writers.

What follows has grown out of three lectures I delivered to the Princeton Seminar on Jews and Judaism in 1975. This conference is an annual gathering for teachers at the college or seminary level sponsored jointly by the Anti-Defamation League of B'nai B'rith and Princeton Theological Seminary. My special thanks go to Rabbis Solomon S. Bernards and Leon Klenicki of B'nai B'rith, who have offered me steady encouragement to expand the lectures for publication. I am also grateful to those other participants in the 1975 conference whose careful responses helped me to clarify my own thinking. I remember particularly my former colleagues, Professors J. Christiaan Beker of Princeton Seminary and Donald Juel, now of Luther Seminary, St. Paul; Dr. Hayim Gevaryahu, General Secretary of the World Jewish Bible Society; and Rabbi Hershel Matt of Highland Park, New Jersey, the teacher of us all. Whatever obscurities and errors still adhere to this work are of course my own responsibility.

                                                                                J. K.

Pentecost, 1979
Chelsea Square
New York City

Jews and Christians in Dialogue:

New Testament Foundations

CHAPTER 1

Jesus and the First Church:
At Home in Judaism

THE DEVELOPMENT
OF THE SYNOPTIC TRADITION

Our purpose is to determine Jesus' attitude toward Jews and Judaism. That, however, is no easy task. Today, when scholars want to study any particular theme in the ministry of Jesus, they investigate the "Synoptic tradition." This is a catchall term for the contents of Matthew, Mark, and Luke *plus* the history of this material prior to the written form it assumes in the three Gospels. Why must scholars interested in Jesus' ministry be concerned with the *entire history* of this Gospel material? The following considerations will help to explain.

Our first three Gospels were written between 68 and 90 c.e. (Common Era), thirty-five years or more after the ministry of Jesus.[1] Mark, the shortest and most elementary in terms of Greek style, was probably the earliest of the three. Some of Jesus' sayings and deeds were undoubtedly preserved in writing prior to Mark's Gospel, but unfortunately we now possess none of these pre-New Testament documents. Other traditions survived only through oral retelling. Thus, both orally and in writing, Christians transmitted the sayings and acts of Jesus over a period of several decades. Whenever such transmission takes place, a process of development occurs. Stories and sayings grow longer or shorter. Details are added or dropped. Some features become prominent because the transmitter wishes to make a particular point; others receive less emphasis because they do not seem relevant to the current situation. The style in which a given piece of material is presented undergoes significant change as it passes from one teller to another.

We can illustrate this process of development by examining the story of the rich young man as told in Matthew, Mark, and Luke, placing the three versions of it in parallel columns. (See p. 17.) Our Gospel accounts turn out to be "synoptic" (from two Greek words meaning "seen together with") in the sense that all are telling the same basic story and all place it in approximately the same position within their respective book outlines.[2] Nevertheless, when we look closely at our parallel columns we notice that no two of the stories agree in every detail. Only in Mk. 10:21 does the narrator tell us that Jesus loved the rich man. Only from Mt. 19:21 do we learn that Jesus said, "If you would be perfect. . . ." According to Mk. 10:17f. and Lk. 18:18f., the rich man addresses Jesus as "Good Teacher," and Jesus responds to this flattering title by asking, "Why do you call me good?" In Mt. 19:16 the rich man first encounters Jesus with the question, "Teacher, what good deed must I do, to have eternal life?" and Jesus answers with "Why do you ask me about what is good?"

By observing data like these, scholars can begin to reconstruct the way things may really have happened in the ministry of Jesus. Sometimes they can determine which parts of the story are "early" (that is, close to the ministry of Jesus) and which parts are "late" (that is, modified in the retelling or rewriting). Certainty on these matters is seldom attainable. Historians customarily speak of probabilities. Nevertheless, when common patterns of development begin to emerge from several stories or sayings, the probability factor becomes quite high.

When we try to determine Jesus' attitude toward Jews and Judaism, we shall assume with the majority of Biblical scholars today that the Synoptic tradition was molded during the process of its transmission. In practical terms, this means that not everything on our theme attributed to Jesus in the Synoptic Gospels accurately reflects the real situation in his ministry. At this point we cannot spell out a comprehensive method for distinguishing "early" material from "late" material. Instead, we shall take up questions of method as they arise in our

THE RICH YOUNG MAN

Mt. 19:16-23

16And behold, one came up to him, saying, "Teacher, what good deed must I do to have eternal life?" 17And he said to him, "Why do you ask me about what is good? One there is who is good. If you would enter life, keep the commandments." 18He said to him, "Which?" and Jesus said, "You shall not kill, You shall not commit adultery, You shall not steal, You shall not bear false witness, 19Honor your father and mother, and, You shall love your neighbor as yourself." 20The young man said to him, "All these I have observed; what do I still lack?" 21Jesus said to him, "If you would be perfect, go, sell what you possess; and give to the poor, and you will have treasure in heaven; and come, follow me." 22When the young man heard this he went away sorrowful; for he had great possessions.

23And Jesus said to his disciples, "Truly, I say to you, it will be hard for a rich man to enter the kingdom of heaven."

Mk. 10:17-23

17And as he was setting out on his journey, a man ran up and knelt before him, and asked him, "Good Teacher, what must I do to inherit eternal life?" 18And Jesus said to him, "Why do you call me good? No one is good but God alone. 19You know the commandments: 'Do not kill, Do not commit adultery, Do not steal, Do not bear false witness, Do not defraud, Honor your father and mother.'"

20And he said to him, "Teacher, all these I have observed from my youth." 21And Jesus looking upon him loved him, and said to him, "You lack one thing; go, sell what you have, and give to the poor, and you will have treasure in heaven; and come, follow me." 22At that saying his countenance fell, and he went away sorrowful; for he had great possessions.

23And Jesus looked around and said to his disciples, "How hard it will be for those who have riches to enter the kingdom of God!"

Lk. 18:18-24

18And a ruler asked him, "Good Teacher, what shall I do to inherit eternal life?" 19And Jesus said to him, "Why do you call me good? No one is good but God alone. 20You know the commandments: 'Do not commit adultery, Do not kill, Do not steal, Do not bear false witness, Honor your father and mother.'"

21And he said, "All these I have observed from my youth." 22And when Jesus heard it, he said to him, "One thing you still lack. Sell all that you have and distribute to the poor, and you will have treasure in heaven; and come, follow me." 23But when he heard this he became sad, for he was very rich. 24Jesus looking at him said, "How hard it is for those who have riches to enter the kingdom of God!"

consideration of various sayings and acts of Jesus. We shall sketch our picture of Jesus' ministry largely from material in the Synoptic Gospels. The Fourth Gospel, which is treated separately in Chapter 6, presents a highly stylized portrait of Jesus that requires special attention. On occasion, the Fourth Gospel does offer historical correctives to the Synoptic tradition. Where these occur, we shall point them out.

JESUS' ENVIRONMENT: GALILEE AND THE *HASIDIM*

Today, no one denies that Jesus was a Jew. During the Hitler era one could find perverse attempts by pro-Nazi scholars to prove the contrary. They argued that inasmuch as Jesus came from the remote northern district of Galilee he must have been ethnically different from people who lived down south in the vicinity of Jerusalem, and hence more "Arian" than Jewish. Inevitably, these tendentious efforts failed because they distorted the evidence. Modern research shows that Jews in ancient Galilee were just as Jewish as Jews in Judea. Yet there was a grain of truth in the pro-Nazi arguments, as there is in all demonic propaganda. During the first century, Galilean Jews would probably have stood out in a Jerusalem crowd. For one thing, they spoke Aramaic with a peculiar accent (see Mt. 26:73). For another, Galilean Jews seemed particularly bold and independent in the eyes of their southern brothers and sisters. Modern Jews would perhaps say that they showed plenty of chutzpah.

There are geographical and historical reasons for this distinctiveness. As a territory, Galilee existed in some isolation from the rest of Palestinian Judaism. It was bordered on the north and west by the Roman province of Syria, on the east by Gaulanitis and the Decapolis (both largely pagan in population), and on the south by Samaria, where the inhabitants were regarded by pious folk in Galilee and Judea alike as apostates from Judaism. Consulting a map of first-century Israel gives a pictorial view of the situation. Galilee, it may be seen, represented something of a Jewish island in a sea of non-Jews. Consequently, its religious practices developed along lines somewhat different from those in Judea.[3] For example, the Zealot movement, which embodied the militant anti-Roman position, seems to have originated in Galilee shortly before the time of Jesus. Jews in Judea, under the direct rule of Roman procurators, tended to accommodate themselves, albeit reluctantly, to the superior power of the occupying army. Judeans must have looked to the rebel movement in Galilee with a mixture of admiration, disapproval, and fear.

Apparently, observant Jews in Judea also regarded Galileans as generally unlearned in matters of Torah and somewhat lackadaisical in their practice of ritual piety. Two first-century rabbis from Galilee are criticized in a later Jewish source (the Mishnah) for disregarding customs of acceptable scholarly behavior: one was discovered walking alone at night and the other was found engaging in lengthy conversation with a woman.[4] Another Galilean rabbi, in opposition to the majority opinion, taught that rubbing ears of field grain together for food constituted no violation of the Sabbath.[5] Thus the Judaism of Jesus' home territory stood in a certain tension with the more careful, scholarly Judaism of Judea. Nevertheless—and this point we must emphasize—Galilean Judaism was always in full communion with Judean Judaism. However much the two groups criticized each other, they continued to regard each other as brothers and sisters in religion as well as race. Galileans willingly paid the annual tax to support the Temple worship in Jerusalem and made regular pilgrimages there to celebrate the major festivals. This means that when we read about Jesus' conflicts with Jerusalem Pharisees and other representatives of Judean orthodoxy, the parties in the dispute were not challenging each other's right to exist within Judaism. Disagreements about the interpretation of Torah were common in first-century Judaism, especially between Galileans and Judeans. Yet they hardly ever led to a break in community.

We may examine a phenomenon in the Judaism of Jesus' day which illustrates this "fellowship in conflict." It is the tradition of the *hasid,* or holy man, who irritated religious authorities with his unconventional behavior but ultimately won their respect. One of these figures, Honi by name, lived in the century prior to Jesus and earned his reputation as a rainmaker. The authorities complained that Honi lived on far too intimate terms with God, assailing the Almighty with his requests like a spoiled child badgering his father. Yet Honi's prayers usually received positive answers. Simeon ben Shetah, a leading Pharisee of the time, had no recourse but to admire the *hasid.* "What can I do with you," conceded Simeon, "since even though you importune God, he does what you wish in the same way that a father does whatever his importuning son asks?"[6] The traditions about Honi are associated with Jerusalem, but his grandson, who was also known as a rainmaker and may have been a contemporary of Jesus, appears to have resided in Galilee.[7]

A second *hasid,* who lived shortly after Jesus, was the Galilean rabbi Hanina ben Dosa. Hanina possessed a remarkable ability to heal through prayer. Tradition has it that by means of his intercession the son of the famous Pharisaic teacher Johanan ben Zakkai was cured. Johanan and his fellow rabbinic scholars both respected and resented Hanina's miracle-working power, for they themselves did not possess it. Yet they never questioned its divine origin.[8] Nor do we find any evidence to suggest that Hanina condemned them for their ambivalence toward him, or challenged their positions as religious leaders of Israel. Healers and teachers stood in a complementary (if not always harmonious) relationship in first-century Judaism.

Our purpose in referring to these two early *hasidim* has been to show that the Judaism of Jesus' environment allowed for a great deal of diversity. Inasmuch as Jesus was both a Galilean and a hasidic healer, he undoubtedly raised eyebrows among the more orthodox religious authorities, particularly since he had not studied with any of them. Thus, a degree of conflict between the two was almost inevitable. But Jewish tradition suggests that differences over Torah interpretation and personal behavior would not in themselves lead to official condemnation by the authorities. We Christians must resist the conventional opinion that all, or even most, of the religious leaders in Israel devoted themselves to doing away with Jesus.

JESUS AND THE RELIGIOUS AUTHORITIES

But how did Jesus feel toward *them?* The Synoptic Gospels are filled with accounts of controversial encounters between Jesus and various groups of scribes and Pharisees. These include stories about the healing and forgiving of a paralyzed man (Mt. 9:1–8//Mk. 2:1–12//Lk. 5:17–26); Jesus' disciples plucking ears of grain on the Sabbath (Mt. 12:1–8//Mk. 2:23–28//Lk. 6:1–5); Jesus' healing of a man with a withered hand, also on the Sabbath (Mt. 12:9–14//Mk. 3:1–6//Lk. 6:6–11); the so-called Beelzebul controversy in which Jesus defends himself against accusations that he exorcises demons with the aid of demons (Mt. 12:22–37//Mk. 3:20–30); a debate about fasting and table fellowship with tax collectors and prostitutes (Mt. 9:9–17//Mk. 2:13–22//Lk. 5:27–39); an argument over ritual and moral purity in which Jesus criticizes some religious leaders for valuing tradition more highly than the Ten Commandments (Mt. 15:1–20//Mk. 7:1–23); a discussion about Jesus' authority to cleanse the Temple (Mt. 21:23–27//Mk. 11:27–33//Lk. 20:1–8); and controversies centering on the payment of taxes, the resurrection, the greatest commandment in the Torah, and the Davidic sonship of the Messiah (Mt. 22:15–46//Mk. 12:13–37//Lk. 20:22–44).

In all these Gospel accounts Jesus emerges from the disputes as a clear winner. On grounds of probability alone we must wonder whether the original battles turned out quite so one-sided. But the noteworthy point for our inquiry is that none of these controversies would have seemed abnormal in the Judaism of Jesus' day. Arguments about the interpretation of Torah and tradition went on all the time. Challenges to the behavior of popular figures, especially by religious authorities, and responses to those challenges by the persons involved were commonplace. Generally such controversies did not imply an unbridgeable break in community between the opposing parties. They formed a natural part of the give-and-take of first-century Judaism.

More important, there is nothing in the Gospel stories listed above to suggest that Jesus considered himself beyond the authority of the scribes, Pharisees, or Sadducees. Though he took positions against them on specific matters of interpretation and behavior, he never condemned them wholesale or declared their leadership illegitimate. Luke tells us that Jesus expressed his desire for intimacy with Pharisees in the same way he expressed it with tax collectors and sinners —by eating with them (Lk. 7:36ff.; 11:37ff.; 14:1ff.). According to Matthew, Jesus told the crowds that followed him, along with his own disciples: "The scribes and the Pharisees sit on Moses' seat; so practice and observe whatever they tell you" (Mt. 23:2-3). Both of these details probably correspond to the actual facts of Jesus' ministry; for the early church, in its growing conflict with Judaism (see Chapters 3-6), is not likely to have created them.

Yet we do find some material in the Gospels which shows Jesus delivering comprehensive denunciations of the scribes and Pharisees. This we need to examine in some detail. One group of passages describes the request of the scribes and Pharisees for a sign from Jesus. This request seems natural enough and appears to be made in good faith. In replying to it, Jesus states bluntly that "an evil and adulterous generation seeks for a sign; but no sign shall be given to it except the sign of the prophet Jonah," i.e., Jonah's call for repentance (Mt. 12:38-39; 16:1-4; in Lk. 11:29 Jesus' response is made to "the crowds"). This sounds like a blanket condemnation of Jesus' hearers. But there is good reason to believe that Jesus was really not so harsh in judging the religious leaders' request for a sign as Matthew suggests. In Mark's version of the same story, Jesus responds to the Pharisees' question with a deep sigh accompanied by the words: "Why does this generation seek a sign? Truly, I say to you, no sign shall be given to this generation" (Mk. 8:11-13). This simple, spontaneous reply expresses frustration but does not condemn the entire generation. It is probably closer to what Jesus actually said. The more developed versions in Matthew and Luke must reflect a time when the church found growing resistance to its gospel on the part of Jews.

Among the other stories and sayings in which Jesus acts as a critic of the religious leaders, none is more problematical for Jewish-Christian relations today than Mt. 23:3b-36 and its parallel in Lk. 11: 37-52. For Jews, some of the most offensive judgments in the entire New Testament occur here. Christians need to remember that today's Jews claim the Pharisees as their spiritual ancestors. We may then be able to understand something of what our elder brothers and sisters feel when they encounter words like these, attributed to Jesus by the Gospel writers:

> The scribes and the Pharisees . . . preach, but do not practice. They bind heavy burdens, hard to bear, and lay them on men's shoulders; but they themselves will not move them with their finger. They do all their deeds to be seen by men, . . . and they love the place of honor at feasts and the best seats in the synagogues, and salutations in the market places, and being called rabbi by men. . . .
>
> But woe to you, scribes and Pharisees, hypocrites! Because you shut the kingdom of heaven against men; for you neither enter yourselves, nor allow those who would enter to go in. Woe to you, scribes and Pharisees, hypocrites! for you traverse sea and land to make a single proselyte, and when he becomes a proselyte, you make him twice as much a child of hell as yourselves. . . .
>
> Woe to you, scribes and Pharisees, hypocrites! for you build the tombs of the prophets and adorn the monuments of the righteous, saying, "If we had lived in the days of our fathers, we would not have taken part with them in shedding the blood of the prophets." Thus you witness against yourselves, that you are sons of those who murdered the prophets. Fill up, then, the measure of your fathers. You serpents, you brood of vipers, how are you to escape being sentenced to hell? (Mt. 23, *passim*)

While [Jesus] was speaking, a Pharisee asked him to dine with him; so he went in and sat at table. The Pharisee was astonished to see that he did not first wash before dinner. And the Lord said to him, "Now you Pharisees cleanse the outside of the cup and of the dish, but inside you are full of extortion and wickedness. You fools! Did not he who made the outside make the inside also? But give for alms those things which are within; and behold, everything is clean for you.

"But woe to you, Pharisees! for you tithe mint and rue and every herb, and neglect justice and the love of God; these you ought to have done, without neglecting the others. . . ."

One of the lawyers answered him, "Teacher, in saying this you reproach us also." And he said, "Woe to you lawyers also! for you load men with burdens hard to bear, and you yourselves do not touch the burdens with one of your fingers. . . . Woe to you lawyers! for you have taken away the key of knowledge; you did not enter and you hindered those who were entering." (Lk. 11, *passim*)

Even to Christians, these "words of Jesus" probably come as a shock. Although many of us learned as children to equate the word "Pharisee" with "hypocrite," most of us now shudder at the New Testament evidence for such a massive generalization.

In an effort to put the best possible construction on these words, one Jewish scholar has pointed out that the rabbinical writers themselves sometimes take a critical view of the Pharisees. According to David Flusser,

> All the motifs of Jesus' famous invective against the Pharisees in Matthew xxiii are also found in rabbinical literature. Both in Jesus' diatribe and in the self-criticism of the rabbis the central polemical motif is the description of the Pharisees as being prone to hypocrisy. Jesus says that "they make up heavy loads and lay them on men's shoulders, but they will not stir a finger to remove them!" (Matthew xxiii, 4). In the Talmud we read about five types of Pharisaic hypocrisy: the first is to "lay the commandments upon men's shoulders" (J. Berakhoth 14b).[9]

But we need to say more. Historians of the first century have shown that by and large the Pharisees were moderate, reasonable people. To be sure, they recommended a strict observance of Torah, and some of them looked with disdain on the uneducated common folk (the so-called *'am ha'aretz,* or "people of the land") who showed no interest in the finer points of the law. But it is surely unfair to condemn Pharisees wholesale as hypocrites, religious exhibitionists, legalistic oppressors, and persecutors of the prophets. Indeed, the Pharisaic movement itself had suffered considerable persecution at the hands of impious rulers in the first century B.C.E. (Before the Common Era). It would in fact be wrong to conclude that Pharisees represented the "establishment" in Judaism at the time of Jesus. According to the first-century Jewish writer Josephus, only six thousand of them lived in the entire land of Palestine. They were outnumbered by their rivals the Sadducees on the Sanhedrin in Jerusalem. As we shall see, they play no role at all in the Gospel accounts of the legal proceedings against Jesus.

Without doubt, some scribes and Pharisees did act in a hypocritical way, and Jesus certainly condemned this, as he condemned hypocritical behavior on the part of his own followers (Mt. 7:21–23; 25:31–46). But the lengthy maledictions heaped upon scribes and Pharisees in Matthew 23 and Luke 11 do not accurately reflect Jesus' real attitude toward them. Most likely, they represent incidents in the ministry of Jesus which received editorial expansion by the Gospel writers when controversy between Judaism and the church came to a head after 70 c.e. Mark 12:38–40, probably written prior to 70, is a shorter, milder version of Matthew 23 and Luke 11. But it applies to scribes only, not Pharisees. In addition, early layers of the Synoptic tradition give us small glimpses of more friendly relationships between Jesus and the religious authorities. Luke tells us, for example, that a group of Pharisees, fearing for Jesus' life, warned him that Herod was plotting against him and urged him to leave Galilee (Lk. 13:31). In Mk. 12:28–34 we read that when a scribe praised Jesus' teaching on the great commandment in the Torah, "Jesus saw that he answered wisely [and] said to him, 'You are not far from the kingdom of God.' "

JESUS ON TORAH, PEOPLE, AND TEMPLE

For Jews, Torah has always meant not simply "law" in the ceremonial or moral sense but the whole revelation of God delivered to Moses on Sinai, including the many stories of God's mercy toward his people. Thus, it should come as no surprise that Jesus affirms the Torah. According to Matthew, he said:

Think not that I have come to abolish the law and the prophets; I have come not to abolish them but to fulfil them. For truly, I say to you, till heaven and earth pass away, not an iota, not a dot, will pass from the law until all is accomplished. Whoever then relaxes one of the least of these commandments and teaches men so, shall be called least in the kingdom of heaven; but he who does them and teaches them shall be called great in the kingdom of heaven. (Mt. 5:17–19)

Some scholars, mostly Protestants, have argued that because this saying occurs only in Matthew, a Gospel whose writer endeavors to make the Messiah into a new Moses, Jesus himself never endorsed the Torah quite so enthusiastically. On the other hand, a partial parallel to Mt. 5:17ff. appears in Luke:

> But it is easier for heaven and earth to pass away, than for one dot of the law to become void. (Lk. 16:17)

Moreover, the opinion that Jesus took a loose view of the Torah can be countered by the simple fact that the first church in Jerusalem obeyed not only the moral but also the ceremonial laws (see Acts 2:1, 46; 3:1). These earliest believers, who included Jesus' own disciples and relatives, understood that he did not mean to abolish the law. In fact, some of the Gospel sayings show Jesus actually heightening the demands of Torah (Mt. 5:21–48; Mk. 10:2–9). Jesus' emphasis on love as the center of the Torah by no means softened the moral requirements laid upon his followers (see Mt. 5:43). Only in Mk. 7:17–23 does Jesus seem to be moving outside the range of a Torah obedience acceptable to the observant Jews of his day. There he is portrayed as abolishing the kosher food laws. Indeed, according to the Gospel writer's editorial comment, "he declared all foods clean" (Mk. 7:19). But this interpretation is probably a Marcan misunderstanding of Jesus' words, for in Acts 10:1–16, we read that the cleanliness of all foods comes as new information revealed sometime after the resurrection in a heavenly vision to a skeptical Peter. Jesus surely skated along the edge of first-century tradition by healing on the Sabbath, eating with "impure" people such as tax collectors and prostitutes, and minimizing the importance of ritual fasts and washings. But only the strictest Pharisees would have seen these deviations as disobedience to Torah itself. The overwhelming weight of evidence requires us to conclude that Jesus respected and upheld all the Torah commandments.

Moreover, it seems clear that Jesus thought of his Jewish brothers and sisters as God's elect people. They, not the Gentiles, were the chief beneficiaries of his ministry. Though he occasionally healed non-Jews, he apparently understood that he had been sent first of all

for Israel's sake (Mt. 15:24). The Canaanite woman who seeks healing for her daughter receives a surprisingly harsh answer from Jesus:
"It is not fair to take the children's bread and throw it to the dogs"
(Mt. 15:26; Mk. 7:27). When a demon-possessed Gentile is exorcised
by Jesus and asks permission to follow him as a disciple, Jesus refuses,
commanding the man instead to return to his home and friends (Mk.
5:18f.; Lk. 8:38f.). In sending the twelve disciples out to preach and
heal, Jesus tells them: "Go nowhere among the Gentiles, and enter
no town of the Samaritans, but go rather to the lost sheep of the
house of Israel" (Mt. 10:5–6; see also Rom. 15:8).

What are we to make of this phrase "the lost sheep of the house
of Israel"? Did Jesus consider all Jews to be lost? Probably so, in the
sense that he thought of them as wandering like "sheep without a
shepherd" (Mt. 9:36; Mk. 6:34). According to Jesus, *everyone* needed
to "repent," that is, turn around, acknowledge the nearness of God's
Kingdom, seek it, and finally enter it. Repentance meant tasting
God's love anew. Even this understanding of one's need to return to
God proves troublesome to modern Jews reading the New Testament. It seems to imply that only Jesus could open people's minds
and hearts to God's Kingdom, that the Judaism of his day was so
ineffective as to offer no resources for discerning God's will. It is
difficult to tell exactly what Jesus taught on this score. He must have
believed that his ministry was introducing something novel into Judaism, though the "new wine in new wineskins" passage (Mt. 9:14–17;
Mk. 2:18–22; Lk. 5:33–39) really applies only to the fasting traditions
of the Pharisees and can in no way be read as a declaration of Judaism's obsolescence. Jesus did take a position against the Temple of
his day, condemning its misuse in the words of the prophets Isaiah
and Jeremiah: "My house shall be called a house of prayer, but you
make it a den of robbers" (Is. 56:7 and Jer. 7:11 in Mt. 21:13 and
parallels). But this charge stands in the tradition of other efforts by
Jewish people through the ages to renew their institutions.

Taken as a whole, the evidence that Jesus presumed a special status
under God for the Jewish people remains most impressive. As we
have seen, Jesus upholds the authority of the Torah and even the
legitimacy of its Pharisaic interpreters (Mt. 23:1–3). For Jesus, lost-

ness does not imply that Jews are cut off from God and without hope. Repentance never means turning to a new religion but rather returning to the God whose mercy is already proclaimed in the traditions and institutions of Judaism. Jesus surely thinks of the people to whom he ministers as God's chosen people.

But is it not true that Jesus refers to a hardening of "this people's heart" in response to his teaching (Mt. 13:13ff.; Mk. 4:10–12; Lk. 8:9–10)? Does he not hold "this generation" accountable for the blood of prophets, wise men, and scribes (Mt. 23:32–36; Lk. 11: 49–51)? No doubt Jesus did sometimes experience great frustration at the lack of enthusiastic response from his hearers. Almost certainly, he let fly some angry words to express his consternation. The passages above probably echo things said by Jesus on such occasions. But in their present form the sayings have clearly undergone a development in the Synoptic tradition. The hardening motif varies considerably from Matthew to Mark to Luke. Only Matthew, quoting Isaiah, actually speaks of a heart that has grown "dull." Luke's version is relatively mild. It states that while the disciples have received knowledge of the secrets of the Kingdom, "for others [the secrets] are in parables, so that seeing they may not see, and hearing they may not understand" (Lk. 8:10). This text could refer not to the people's lack of response but to an intention on Jesus' part to keep some elements of his teaching temporarily within the private group of his disciples. In any case, it hardly pronounces a final and universal judgment upon the perceptions of the Jewish people.

There are several passages in the Synoptic tradition which refer to "this generation." They range in severity from Jesus' exasperated sigh over the repeated demands of "this generation" for a sign (Mk. 8:11ff.) to denunciations of "this generation" as evil, adulterous, and guilty of all Israel's past sins (Mt. 12:39; 16:4; 17:17; 23:32ff.). Almost certainly, the tradition has developed from mild to harsh. As the church's conflict with Judaism grew in the 70s and 80s, those words of Jesus which criticized Jews were expanded, i.e., transformed from responses to specific situations in his ministry into general statements about all Jews everywhere. Thus, the prophecy that "the kingdom of God will be taken away from you [Jewish leaders] and given to a nation producing the fruits of it" appears only in Mt. 21:43, even though the parable in which it occurs is recorded by all three Synoptic Evangelists! It must have been added later by Matthew as disputes between his church and the synagogue intensified.

Jesus' last trip to Jerusalem probably resulted from a mounting conviction on his part that he must confront Jewish leaders in the Holy City with his message of the Kingdom's imminence. Appropriately enough, he set forth his teaching in the most holy place of Judaism, the Temple (Mt. 26:55; Mk. 14:49; Lk. 22:53). All three Synoptic writers imply that this teaching took place *after* the Temple cleansing (compare Mt. 21:10ff.//Mk. 11:15ff.//Lk. 19:45ff. with Mt. 21:23ff.; Mk. 11:27ff.; Lk. 20:1ff.). If this presentation of the sequence is historically accurate, Jesus' cleansing of the Temple could not have been a very violent event, for it resulted neither in his arrest nor in his banishment from the Temple precincts. Most likely, the "cleansing" was a prophetic demonstration similar in character to Jeremiah's protest (Jer. 7:1ff.). Like Jeremiah, Jesus also predicted the destruction of the Temple (Mt. 24:1-3; Mk. 13:-1-4; Lk. 21:5-7), though he seems to have uttered this oracle privately to his disciples, not aloud within the Temple itself. Unlike Jeremiah, Jesus did not tie the destruction of the Temple specifically to the sins of the people (Jer. 7:16-20). He may have made his prediction on the basis of special revelation, or he may have simply discerned that revolutionary forces already at work in his native Galilee (e.g., the militant Zealot movement) would force the country into a military confrontation with Rome which would result in Jerusalem's inevitable destruction. At any rate, Jesus did not pronounce the Temple itself valueless from a religious point of view.[10] Otherwise, his first followers in Jerusalem would not have continued to worship there after the resurrection (Acts 2:46; 3:1; 5:12, 25). As a matter of fact, Jesus showed more optimism about the Temple's immediate future than Jeremiah. His act of cleansing it suggests that a certain rehabilitation might occur even prior to its destruction. Jeremiah simply delivered a message of unrelieved doom against it (Jer. 7:16-20).

JESUS' MISSION

Did Jesus believe that his ministry would reform Judaism as a whole? "Reform" is probably not the right word, for Jesus seems to have expected his work to usher in the Kingdom of God on earth (Mt. 12:28//Lk. 11:20; Mk. 13:30; 14:25). If the coming of the Kingdom was imminent, no time remained for a full-scale national reformation. Still, as we have seen, Jesus hardly felt that the approaching Kingdom rendered obsolete the commands of Torah, God's special election of the Jewish people, or even the Temple. Jesus demanded repentance, but this was a repentance within the traditions of Judaism, not repentance *from* Judaism. The fact that Jesus chose twelve disciples has been seen by some scholars as a parabolic announcement that he was beginning to reassemble the ancient tribes for the renewal of all Israel. In the hours just prior to his arrest, Jesus demonstrated a deep loyalty to the traditions and hopes of his people. His words over the cup at the Last Supper have probably been transmitted more accurately in Mark and Matthew ("This is my blood of the covenant . . .," Mt. 26:28//Mk. 14:24) than in 1 Cor. 11:25 ("This cup is the *new* covenant in my blood," italics added). Jesus intended to fulfill *the* covenant made with Israel. It was never his purpose to overturn the promises God had made to his people from of old, but rather, to bring them into final realization.

Perhaps then the right word for Jesus' mission is "preparation."[11] Jesus wanted the people of God to rouse themselves, to look longingly for the coming Kingdom, and even to experience joyful foretastes of it. In delivering his message, Jesus criticized his brother and sister Jews. But above all, he sought to tell them the good news that they, precisely as Jews, could expect a decisive intervention of God on their behalf. Jesus' lament over Jerusalem (Mt. 23:37–39; Lk. 13:34–35) is best understood as a hope on his part that at this intervention he himself would be welcomed by all Israel as one "who comes in the name of the Lord."

JESUS' DEATH

It was to be expected that some elements within Judaism, and the Roman procurator Pilate as well, would perceive Jesus' ministry as a threat. Thanks to several excellent works by contemporary scholars, it has become almost common knowledge by now that not Pharisees but Sadducean high priests and Romans played the chief role in bringing about Jesus' execution.[12] Those who put Jesus to death apparently feared that if his Kingdom teaching were allowed to continue, it might raise the hopes of the common people to fever pitch. The authorities no doubt supposed, perhaps rightly, that revolutionaries would take advantage of heightened expectations by urging people to shorten the days of the worldly kingdom through acts of political rebellion. In the unstable Palestine of the 30s such a situation could well have developed into open war between Jewish patriots and the Roman legions stationed in Jerusalem and Caesarea. The writer of the Fourth Gospel is probably quite accurate in reporting, if not the actual words, then surely the thoughts of the high priest Caiaphas concerning Jesus: "It is expedient for you that one man should die for the people, and that the whole nation should not perish" (Jn. 11:50). No Pharisee spoke those words. Ironically, the Pharisees, who debated with Jesus most heatedly over his interpretation of Torah and his personal behavior, played no significant role in condemning him to death.[13] We Christians need to say this with force, both to ourselves and to modern Jews, the spiritual descendants of the Pharisees. The fact that these ancient Jews were innocent helps to set the Gospel accounts of Jesus' trial and death into clearer perspective for Jewish-Christian dialogue today.

THE JERUSALEM CHURCH AS SAVING REMNANT

It was nothing less than remarkable that the earliest church in Jerusalem and the Judaism of Jerusalem did not reject each other wholesale. From the church's side, it was a bold decision to settle in the city where Jesus had met his death. For all these earliest believers knew, they might suffer the same fate. That they chose to remain demonstrates their obedience to Jesus' command: "Take up [your] cross and follow me" (Mk. 8:34). At the same time, however, their decision also shows a continuing commitment to Judaism. They were convinced that the good news of the resurrection had to be preached *to Israel,* especially to the Jews of Jerusalem, where the Messiah was expected to reappear. If the church feared Judaism's authorities, it did not manifest that fear in the earliest days, for it refused to become an underground organization. Members of the church preached about Jesus in public and even attended Temple worship as a group (Acts 2:46). We have no evidence that they differed from their Jewish brothers and sisters in observance of the moral and ceremonial commandments. However, in their proclamation of Jesus as the Christ, in their call for national repentance, in their conviction that the Holy Spirit dwelt among them, in their house gatherings for table fellowship, in their healings, in their belief that the last days had come upon humankind, they stood out plainly from other Jews.

We must also marvel at the decision of the authorities to allow the church a relatively free rein in Jerusalem. Luke reports that the high priests and Sadducees in the Sanhedrin (but not the Pharisees!) did try to muzzle the preaching of the first believers. But this attempt failed, we are told, because the common people supported church members and because a moderate Pharisee named Gamaliel persuaded the council that believers in Jesus had a right to exist within Judaism (Acts 4:21; 5:26, 33–42). Whether or not the reasons Luke gives for the council's decision are completely accurate, some kind of live-and-let-live policy must have evolved between official Judaism and church. Moreover, this policy seems to have remained fairly stable. The church existed as a public institution in Jerusalem from Pentecost until the early 60s, when its leader, James the brother of Jesus, suffered martyrdom at the hands of an ambitious high priest. Periodically, selective persecutions of the church occurred, for political reasons no doubt. The most severe took place in connection with Stephen and the Hellenists. But not even this pressure caused the church to abandon its public preaching.

How did the church understand itself, and what did it hope to accomplish? Almost certainly, the church viewed itself as a saving remnant within Judaism. It behaved as an enlightened circle whose task was to enlarge itself by spreading the word. It felt gifted and wished to share this gift—but only with Jews, who as God's elect constituted the logical recipients of his good favor. In two missionary sermons, attributed by Luke to Peter, we find these words:

> For the promise is to you [Jews] and to your children and to all that are far off, every one whom the Lord our God calls to him [from the Diaspora]. (Acts 2:39)

> You [Jews] are the sons of the prophets and of the covenant which God gave to your fathers, saying to Abraham, "And in your posterity shall all the families of the earth be blessed." God, having raised up his servant, sent him to you first, to bless you in turning every one of you from your wickedness. (Acts 3:25f.)

Like Jesus, the church denounced sin and called for repentance. Indeed, it even charged the common people with indirect responsibility for the death of Jesus (Acts 2:23). According to Luke, Peter exhorted his hearers to "save yourselves from this crooked generation" (2:40). By and large, however, the emphasis in this early Jerusalem preaching, as presented in Acts, fell not on the people's sin, which was after all committed in ignorance, but on the benefits of repentance. Again, from the two sermons attributed to Peter:

> Repent, and be baptized every one of you in the name of Jesus Christ for the forgiveness of your sins; and you shall receive the gift of the Holy Spirit. (Acts 2:38)

> And now, brethren, I know that you acted in ignorance, as did also your rulers. But what God foretold by the mouth of all the prophets, that his Christ should suffer, he thus fulfilled. Repent therefore, and turn again, that your sins may be blotted out, that times of refreshing may come from the presence of the Lord [God], and that he may send the Christ appointed for you, Jesus, whom heaven must receive until the time for establishing all that God spoke by the mouth of his holy prophets from of old. (Acts 3:17–21)

In reporting that the church preached more about good news than about the guilt of people and rulers, Luke must be substantially correct. Otherwise, the authorities would not have tolerated this sect within the boundaries of Judaism. The church, for its part, must have continued to view the Jerusalem Jews among whom it lived as God's people. It did not give up on them, as the inhabitants of Qumran had done; it never moved out to a desert monastery to keep itself pure and aloof from "sinners." Indeed, the Jerusalem church worked to enlarge Israel. When Gentiles began to believe in Jesus as Lord and Christ, the mother church exerted all the influence it could muster to judaize them (see Gal. 2:11–16 and Acts 15:1–35; 21:17–25). In doing so, it probably acted not only out of self-interest—its existence in Jerusalem would surely be threatened if ritually impure Gentiles took part in its table fellowship and worship—but also out of a desire to transmit Israel's heritage to the newcomers. For the church of Jerusalem was first and last a *Jewish* community.

STEPHEN CREATES A SCHISM

Yet the earliest church did not always agree on how Jesus should be interpreted to the inhabitants of Jerusalem. Among its members were a number of Greek-speaking Jews who distinguished themselves from the Palestinian majority. One of them, Stephen, seems to have laid a particularly heavy load of guilt on the Jewish leaders. In the Acts 7 speech attributed to him by Luke, he denounces the Sanhedrin not only for its part in Jesus' execution (the historicity of which may be questioned) but also for the more or less constant apostasy of its predecessors. According to Stephen, Jewish leaders in general had regularly rejected God's emissaries and had never really observed the law (Acts 7:51–53).

After arousing the anger of his hearers with such blanket judgments, Stephen then proceeds to condemn the Temple as a mistake from the very beginning. According to him, God gave Moses directions for the construction of a *tabernacle,* but it was a human being, Solomon, who undertook to build the Temple. Therefore, the very existence of such a building violated God's will (Acts 7:44–50). In Acts 6:13f., Stephen's detractors complain that he is preaching about a Jesus who will come to destroy the Temple in person and change the customs inherited from Moses. Luke calls these detractors "false witnesses" (6:13) but never sets forth an explicit rebuttal of their charge. Thus Stephen comes across as a "radical" within the earliest church who suffers a martyr's death for his boldness. His execution triggers a widespread persecution of the church during which those believers who sided with him had to flee Jerusalem. But according to Luke, the twelve apostles, who presumably did not take Stephen's extreme position, remained in the city (8:1). On the one hand, Luke wants to show that the church honored its first martyr ("Devout men buried Stephen, and made great lamentation over him," 8:2). At the same time, however, he implies that the chief officers of the Jerusalem church would never have preached against Jewish leaders as Stephen did.

Only later, when Peter had identified himself with a "liberal" element in the church which encouraged the Gentile mission (see Acts 10 and 11), did he suffer the threat of death in Jerusalem. At this time, Herod actually executed one of the twelve, James the son of Zebedee. Peter, imprisoned shortly thereafter, escaped the king's clutches with angelic help and fled the city both for his own safety and that of the church (12:1–17). Outside Judea, the church underwent great changes. Gentiles flooded its ranks, and Jewish members in the mixed congregations of Asia Minor and Europe became less careful in their observance of the ancient customs. But in Jerusalem the church remained steadfastly and devoutly Jewish.

This divergence of practice in the earliest church raises a question that modern Christians have not faced squarely. Is the Jerusalem church's desire to maintain its life within Judaism of any consequence in forming contemporary Christian thought? In searching for an answer, we must reckon with the fact that even the apostle Paul, another radical by Jerusalem standards, worked vigorously to achieve reconciliation with this mother of all churches (Rom. 15:25–31).

CONCLUSION

Jesus and the Jerusalem church preached the imminent coming of God's final redemption. In doing so, they criticized certain practices in the Judaism of their day. They demanded repentance from all, for they believed that because of God's new acts in the ministry of Jesus, Israel could no longer carry on business as usual. Yet the new salvation they proclaimed was a salvation of and within Judaism. Its images of redemption came directly from Jewish Scripture and tradition. The validity of Torah, the election of the Jewish people, and (generally) the sanctity of the Temple were upheld.

Inevitably, conflicts arose between new movement and establishment. The really surprising fact, however, is that these two groups arrived at a way of living with each other in the very city where Jesus had met his death. Both believing and nonbelieving Jews recognized, however much it strained their theological sensibilities, that the other party still held membership in the one people of God. At this stage of their mutual history Jesus' acts and teachings, as well as the community of believers that sprang from them, could claim a legitimate home in Judaism.

This time of origins, which we consider normative for Christian life today in many respects, has been slighted as a resource for the church's relationship with Judaism. Since the record of these first years has found its way into the New Testament canon, is it not in some sense prescriptive for contemporary Christian thinking about Jews and Judaism? To state the matter sharply: Can we Gentile Christians of today forget all about the Judaism that was fundamental to the faith of the earliest church?

CHAPTER 2

Paul: On the Way to Unity

PAUL'S PLACE
IN THE HISTORY OF THE CHURCH

Some Jewish and Christian scholars have identified Paul as the real "founder" of Christianity.[1] By employing this bold title, they claim that while the Jerusalem church kept well within the boundaries of Judaism, Paul, the chief apostle to the Gentiles, strayed far from Palestinian thinking and practice—so far, in fact, that he actually inaugurated a religion essentially different from that espoused by Jesus and the first believers.

Such scholars rightly point out that Paul goes beyond the Synoptic Gospels in speaking of Jesus' preexistence (2 Cor. 8:9; Phil. 2:5ff.) and his participation with God the Father in the creation of the world (1 Cor. 8:6; Col. 1:15–20). In contrast to the earliest church, Paul scarcely mentions the sayings and acts of the historical Jesus. Nor does the Kingdom of God, a central theme in Jesus' preaching, receive much attention in the Pauline letters. Instead, Paul focuses on the Kingdom of *Christ*, which for him consists of the Lord's victorious struggle with the powers of this age from the vantage of his heavenly throne (1 Cor. 15:20ff.), and his simultaneous presence through the Spirit in the hearts of believers (Rom. 8:9–11). By means of Baptism and the Lord's Supper, Paul teaches, believers are joined with Jesus' death and resurrection in a sacramental way (Rom. 6: 1–11; 1 Cor. 10:14–22; 11:23–32; Col. 2:12–20). Through faith, they

37

share in his messianic Kingdom. So intimate is the relationship between Christ and believers that the church can be called his body (1 Cor. 12:12–27). All these facts, say the Paul-as-founder scholars, show that the apostle has substantially altered the simple Jewish faith of Jesus and the early church.

Today, however, an emerging majority of scholars hold that much of what appears in the letters of Paul to be so new and different from Jerusalem Christianity was already brewing in the mind of the church even before Paul's conversion, itself just two or three years after the crucifixion of Jesus.[2] It is becoming clearer that we ought neither to praise nor to condemn Paul as the inventor of early Christian theology. The doctrines of Christ's preexistence, his co-creation of the world, his presence with believers in the Spirit, and so forth, had probably entered Christian thinking soon after the resurrection, many years before Paul wrote his letters. Even the sacramental understanding of believer's participation in Jesus' death and resurrection appears to be pre-Pauline.

To be sure, the apostle elaborated upon these ideas, especially when he attempted to explain them to Gentiles who had little knowledge of Judaism. In the course of these explanations, the ideas themselves sometimes took on a more Hellenistic hue. Yet we go astray if we try to understand Paul as a Hellenist. His view of himself and of the world was not finally derived either from the philosophical schools of Stoicism and Neoplatonism or from the popular thinking about cult gods which shows up in the Greco-Roman mystery religions. When Paul talks about his moorings, he boasts of his Jewish heritage and his learning in Judaism (Gal. 1:14; Phil. 3:5f.). Even after his conversion, he continues to think of himself as a Jew (2 Cor. 11:21–26; Rom. 11:1, 13f.). Increasingly, contemporary scholars are discovering how much Paul's conceptualizing and style of argumentation owe to the traditions of rabbinic Judaism.[3] And to this we must add a striking fact: Paul urges those Gentile believers with whom he corresponds toward full communion with the conservative Jewish church at Jerusalem. Paul regards neither himself nor the Gentile Christians of the Hellenistic world as superior to believers in the mother church. Thus he writes to the Romans:

> I hope to see you in passing as I go to Spain, and to be sped on my journey there by you, once I have enjoyed your company for a little. At present, however, I am going to Jerusalem with aid for the saints. For Macedonia and Achaia [i.e., the congregations in and around Philippi and Corinth] have been pleased to make some contribution for the poor among the saints at Jerusalem; they were pleased to do it, and indeed they are in debt to them, for if the Gentiles have come to share in their spiritual blessings, they ought also to be of service to them in material blessings. . . . I appeal to you, brethren, by our Lord Jesus Christ and by the love of the Spirit, to strive together with me in your prayers to God on my behalf, that I may be delivered from the unbelievers in Judea, and that my service for Jerusalem may be acceptable to the saints, so that by God's will I may come to you with joy and be refreshed in your company. (Rom. 15:24–32)

It is not for the sake of unity and good order alone that Paul desires cordial relationships between Gentiles and the Jerusalem church. Indeed, he frankly states that all Gentile congregations owe a large debt to the mother church. He sees his own mission among the nations as a mediation of the spiritual blessings first granted to believers in Jerusalem. On this level, at least, Paul considers his Christian faith and that of his Gentile converts to be a *Jewish* Christian faith.

But the passage from Romans strikes a further note. In it Paul expresses fear of those Jews in Judea whom he calls "unbelievers." Apparently, he does not feel at ease with them in the people of God. Though never denying their Jewishness, he seems to consider them so different from himself as to be threatening. The distance between Paul and Judaism is also expressed in passages such as the following:

> For you have heard of my *former* life in Judaism, how I persecuted the church of God violently and tried to destroy it. (Gal. 1:13, italics added)

> If any . . . man thinks he has reason for confidence in the flesh, I have more: circumcised on the eighth day, of the people of Israel, of the tribe of Benjamin, a Hebrew born of Hebrews; as to the law a Pharisee, as to zeal a persecutor of the church, as to righteousness under the law blameless. But whatever gain I had, I counted as loss for the sake of Christ. Indeed I count

everything as loss because of the surpassing worth of knowing Christ Jesus my Lord. For his sake I have suffered the loss of all things, and count them as refuse, in order that I may gain Christ. (Phil. 3:4–8)

What shall we conclude? Is Paul a Jew or not? Is he a Jew who thinks that the practice of Judaism no longer matters after Christ's advent? Or has he not quite resolved this issue? Does he protest too much in boasting that he counts all of his "gain" in Judaism as loss for the sake of Christ? These questions require answers. We shall be wrestling with them as we take a closer look at the Pauline writings.

THE ESCHATOLOGICAL FOUNDATION OF PAUL'S THOUGHT

Paul agreed with the Judaism of his day on a most important article of faith. For both, the coming of the Messiah must produce a dramatic change in the *world order*. Paul believed most firmly that Jesus was the Christ. It was Jesus who had appeared to him as the crucified one raised from the dead. It was he who had chosen Paul and commissioned him as apostle to the Gentiles. But precisely because all this had happened, Paul thought, a final shift in the aeons must certainly be taking place. The messianic age was dawning and all sorts of marvelous redemptive events would soon appear on the stage of history. One of these would surely be the general resurrection of the dead. When Paul called Jesus "the first fruits of those who have fallen asleep" (1 Cor. 15:20), he was expressing his belief that, very shortly, others would be raised just as Jesus had been. At the time he wrote 1 Corinthians, Paul expected to witness that event within his own life-span (15:42–52).

Another feature of the messianic Kingdom which was being established in Christ was the spread of the gospel throughout the world. Through the preaching of the good news and the signs and wonders that accompanied it, Paul saw God's Spirit creating a new community (1 Cor. 2:1–4; Gal. 3:2–5). The reconciliation of God and humankind accomplished in Jesus' death was now being offered to all through the proclamation of the apostles (2 Cor. 5:18–21). Moreover, according to Paul, the material world itself would soon take part in the Lord's decisive victory over decay and futility. "With eager longing" creation awaited the imminent return of Jesus as King, for once he had taken up his reign on earth, the final redemption of all matter would follow as a matter of course (Rom. 8:18–23). Paul thought of himself and the church as soldiers in this cosmic struggle. He called the whole flow of divine and human events a "new creation" (2 Cor. 5:17; Gal. 6:15). Paul may have borrowed this term from some noncanonical Jewish writings. In any event, it clearly held a material significance for him. The words which he uses to interpret it in 2 Cor. 5:17 ("the old has passed away, behold, the new has come") allude to the Septuagint translation of Is. 43:18–20, widely used in Paul's day. There the prophet says:

> Do not remember the former things, nor consider the old things. Behold, I am doing new things, which shall now appear. I shall make a way in the wilderness and rivers in the desert. The wild beasts will honor me, the ostriches and sparrows, because I provide water in the wilderness, rivers in the desert, to give drink to my chosen people. (Is. 43:18–20, author's translation)

Like the ancient prophet, Paul expected God to transform not only people but the physical world as well. As the apostle wrote, this had obviously not yet happened; rather, it had just begun to happen through the resurrection of Jesus and the miracles being wrought through his followers. For Paul, the divine-human movement that would soon produce a final spiritual/physical transformation had already broken out on earth. In faith he could claim that "the form of this world is passing away" (1 Cor. 7:31).

Paul sensed that he and the whole world with him stood "between the times." One era was coming to an end; another, the messianic age, was just dawning. Paul's convictions about the state of creation prove foundational for his belief and practice. From them his other thoughts branch out as spokes from the hub of a wheel. We call this central group of assumptions Paul's eschatology, his teachings about the last things.

Many of Paul's brother and sister Jews would have agreed with his picture of these last things. They too thought eschatologically. Like him, they expected the Messiah's coming to initiate a time of physical and spiritual perfection on earth. Judaism tolerated a wide range of beliefs concerning precisely how all this would come to pass, but the essential hope which all Jews held in common was that the Messiah's advent would initiate a cosmic revolution. Of course, the Jewish majority parted company with Paul over his assertion that the messianic age had begun *with Jesus*. Most Jews held that the events Paul proclaimed as messianic were not "worldly" enough to demand their allegiance to the prophet from Nazareth.

But Paul had no doubts about where things stood on God's timetable. To him, it was clear that with the resurrection God had begun to establish his Kingdom on earth in a new way. Even now the principalities and powers of this age were bowing to the reign of Christ (1 Cor. 2:6; 15:23–28). Paul's eschatology produced fundamental changes in his understanding of Judaism, particularly with regard to the status of the Torah. In one of the most provocative statements in the entire New Testament, Paul asserted: "Christ is the end of the law" (Rom. 10:4). What did the apostle mean by this? Unlike most of the early believers in Jesus, Paul was a Pharisee. In affiliating with this party he had concluded that his worth before God depended on his faithful observance of the Torah commands. Consequently, Paul was deeply offended by early Christian believers who, while affirming the Torah's validity, defined their relationship with God through an enlivening experience of the Spirit and a hope that Jesus would soon reappear on earth. Moreover, it did not escape Paul the Pharisee that Gentiles had begun to enter the church. These new believers ignored the strict details of Torah even more than their Jewish brother and sister believers. If Jesus was on their side, thought Paul, then he must surely be the prince of lawbreakers, not the Messiah. Quite logically, Paul became a persecutor of the Jewish church. Jews whose practice threatened to dilute the Torah and confuse the distinction between God's people and the nations were obviously Jews who needed disciplining.

But Paul's conversion turned this reasoning on its head. On the road to Damascus he discovered that Jesus *was* Messiah, and a new syllogism followed: If Jesus, the friend of lawbreakers, had been anointed by God to establish righteousness on earth, then the function of the Mosaic commandments must be reinterpreted. "Now," wrote Paul, "the righteousness of God has been manifested apart from law, although the law and the prophets bear witness to it, the righteousness of God through faith in Jesus Christ for all who believe" (Rom. 3:21–22). It was not that Paul felt impatient to declare the Torah passé because he found it so difficult to obey. Paul never described his conversion as the result of a deficiency in his own Torah zeal or a defectiveness in the Torah itself. Yet his conversion, coupled with his empirical observation that the very righteousness prescribed by Torah was now coming to Gentiles *in the Spirit through faith,* without the observance of circumcision and other ritual commandments, forced him to question whether Torah was the absolute way to righteousness. Eschatology provided the final touch. Paul reasoned that if God had introduced a new path to righteousness *in the last days,* then the old path must be part of a world order that was passing away (1 Cor. 7:31). Hence his bold assertion: "Christ is the end of the law for righteousness to everyone who believes" (Rom. 10:4, author's translation).

Let us note, however, that this claim, radical as it sounds, is carefully circumscribed. Even in the messianic era, Christ does not constitute the end of Torah *for all purposes and for all people.* He is only the end of Torah observance as a path to righteousness, and then, only to those who believe in him as the Christ. Paradoxically, Paul's "antinomian" declaration contains an indirect affirmation of Judaism and the Jewish people! Because of his eschatological assumptions, Paul had to think of Judaism as a path that was passing away, but at the same time he knew that most Jews would not, indeed could not, believe in Jesus' Messiahship prior to his Second Coming. For them, the "old" path to righteousness, Torah observance, must still prevail. Sometimes Paul says disparaging things about this path. We shall examine them shortly. But in Romans, at least, Paul never denies the validity of the Torah path for Jews who cannot accept Jesus as Messiah. "They are Israelites, and to them belong the sonship, the glory, the covenants, the giving of the law, the worship, and the promises" (Rom. 9:4).

Because Paul honors Israel's uniqueness, he makes an astounding concession in Rom. 4:16, a passage usually glossed over by Christian interpreters. From 3:21 through 4:25, Paul is arguing for righteousness by faith, apart for law. To support his argument, he calls as witness (from the Torah!) Abraham, whose faith was reckoned to him as righteousness (4:1ff.). In Paul's view, Abraham is the spiritual forefather of Christians; like him, they receive their righteousness by faith. But now, at the very climax of his argument to establish the new way, Paul pays profound respect to the "old":

> That is why it depends on faith, in order that the promise may rest on grace and be guaranteed to all [Abraham's] descendants—not only to the adherents of the law but also to those who share the faith of Abraham, for he is the father of us all. (Rom. 4:16)

Not only . . . but also! So there are *two* valid ways. Some share the faith of Abraham. Others adhere to the law. Both may claim Abraham as their father. In the final analysis both receive the promise of God by grace. Romans 4:16 puts the "end" of Torah in perspective. It is a sharply restricted end, a carefully qualified "obsolescence." Whatever else Paul intends to say in Rom. 10:4, he does not mean to condemn the orthodox practice of Judaism as contrary to the promises of God. For himself, Paul has counted "as loss for the sake of Christ" all that he gained through the practice of Judaism (Phil. 3:4–11). But he does not thereby assert that Jews who contest Jesus' Messiahship have ceased to worship according to God's will. However much Paul celebrates his own break from Torah practice, his kinship with the Jewish people and their way of Torah remains deep. We Christians violate Paul's intention whenever we portray Judaism as an inauthentic religion.

The apostle's eschatological world view holds yet another surprise for us. We Christians tend to talk about the person and work of Jesus as the fulfillment of Old Testament promises. This language derives from the Gospels, particularly Matthew. In that book, we have noted, Jesus says: "Think not that I have come to abolish the law and the prophets; I have come not to abolish them but to fulfil them" (Mt. 5:17). Matthew frequently interprets events in the ministry of Jesus as fulfillments of Scriptural prophecies. Thus, after narrating the healing of a large group of people by Jesus, the Evangelist writes: "This was to fulfil what was spoken by the prophet Isaiah, 'He took our infirmities and bore our diseases' " (Mt. 8:17; see also 1:22; 4:14f.; 13:14ff.). By contrast, Paul never writes about Jesus and his work as the fulfillment of prophecy! He calls love, not Jesus, the fulfillment of the law (Rom. 13:8; Gal. 5:14). Paul prefers to speak about the relationship between the man from Nazareth and God's ancient promises in another way. In 2 Cor. 1:20 he says of Jesus: "All the promises of God find their Yes in him. That is why we utter the Amen through him, to the glory of God." Jesus' Messiahship represents the decisive affirmation of God's ancient promises. His ministry reinforces belief in their validity. But affirmation and reinforcement are not fulfillment. God's greatest promise of all, the redemption of the entire creation when he becomes "all in all" (1 Cor. 15:28, KJV), has yet to reach its fulfillment. This can happen only when Jesus returns to earth as King (1 Cor. 15:20ff.).

As if to clarify his carefully fashioned position on the relationship between Jesus and God's promises, Paul repeats it, with slight modifications, in Rom. 15:8: "I tell you that Christ became a servant to the circumcised to show God's truthfulness, in order to *confirm* the promises given to the patriarchs" (italics added). The person and work of Jesus dovetail with God's ancient promises. They are of one piece with them, and so they demonstrate God's trustworthiness. Through Jesus, the promises take on additional content. But they still yearn for fulfillment. Creation still groans under the weight of its bondage to futility and decay (Rom. 8:19–22). Therefore, God and his Anointed (not to mention Christians) still have work to do (1 Cor. 15:24–28, 58). Paul remains Jewish enough to take seriously the hard question posed by his brother and sister Jews: If Jesus is Messiah, why doesn't the world look more redeemed? Paul answers that with Jesus' death and resurrection redemption has begun. But redemption is an extended event, a drama still under way. Its most climactic scene has yet to be played out. Thus, Paul carefully refrains from speaking prematurely and falsely about fulfillment.

Paul's eschatological world view, itself shaped by Judaism, forced him to conclude that in Christ, God had initiated a new way to righteousness, apart from Torah observance. For those who believed, Christ was the end of the law! *But only for those who believed.* In its faithful observance of Torah, unbelieving Israel could still claim, with justice, to be living out its vocation as God's beloved people. Paul knew that Israel was interpreting the Scripture correctly when it objected that Jesus' work had not yet accomplished the world's final redemption. True to the Torah and his own Jewish expectations concerning the cosmic blessings of the messianic era, Paul tempered his otherwise radical position with an extremely cautious approach to the fulfillment of God's promises. For Paul, the advent of Christ, new as it was, could never reverse the special election of the Jewish people or render their religious practices and hopes extinct. Such, at any rate, is Paul's mature thinking, as reflected in his letter to the Romans. Shortly, we shall examine that letter in more detail. But first we must confront a number of passages, written earlier in Paul's ministry, which seem at odds with the conclusions just noted.

THE EMBATTLED AND REFLECTIVE PAUL

In 1 Thessalonians, which is probably the earliest of Paul's letters now fixed in the New Testament canon, we find this belligerent message to the apostle's Gentile readers:

> For you, brethren, became imitators of the churches of God in Christ Jesus which are in Judea; for you suffered the same things from your own countrymen as they did from the Jews, who killed both the Lord Jesus and the prophets, and drove us out, and displease God and oppose all men by hindering us from speaking to the Gentiles that they may be saved—so as always to fill up the measure of their sins. But God's wrath has come upon them at last! (1 Thess. 2:14–16)

Needless to say, this passage strikes Jewish readers as altogether hostile. It lays the blame for Jesus' death solely on Jews. The Romans get off scot-free. Moreover, the text seems to link Jesus' death with those of the prophets, with the result that Israel comes across as an apostate nation ever rejecting God's genuine messengers. We can almost detect a vindictive glee in the pronouncement: "God's wrath has come upon them at last!"

How shall we deal with this passage? At least one scholar has argued that it is an interpolation added to the text of 1 Thessalonians after Paul's death by a Christian editor reflecting on the destruction of Jerusalem in 70 C.E.[4] This may be correct, but since there is no manuscript variant supporting the hypothesis, it is probably better to wrestle with the text as we have it. Christians have no need to prove Paul sinless or inerrant. As a convert who had persecuted the church, he naturally harbored strong feelings against his former co-persecutors. For their part, they probably considered him a turncoat.

On the other hand, we need to exercise care so as not to read this passage exclusively in the light of such Gospel accounts as Mt. 23:37, where Jerusalem is condemned as a city which traditionally kills God's messengers, or as the story recorded in Acts 7:51f., where Stephen denounces the Jewish Sanhedrin as

> stiff-necked people, uncircumcised in heart and ears, [who] always resist the Holy Spirit. As your fathers did, so do you. Which of the prophets did not your fathers persecute? And they killed those who announced beforehand the coming of the Righteous One, whom you have now betrayed and murdered. (Acts 7:51–52)

If Paul subscribed to such a wholesale condemnation of Jewish leadership, he does not say so in our text. Since he talks first about Jesus, then about the prophets, and then about "us," it seems likely that the prophets he has in mind are not the ancient prophets but *Christian* prophets such as Stephen.

On this hypothesis, we find no attempt here in 1 Thessalonians, as in Matthew and Acts, to forge a chain of guilt extending far back into Israel's history. The offenses against which Paul protests are limited to specific acts committed in the recent past, partly against himself. He condemns only those Jews who actually took part in the killing of Jesus and the Christian prophets, and in his own expulsion.

If our reasoning is correct, there should be no comma between "Jews" and "who" in verses 14b and 15a. The passage then reads as follows:

> . . . for you suffered the same things from your own countrymen as they did from the Jews who killed both the Lord Jesus and the prophets and drove us out. . . . (1 Thess. 2:14–15)

Given Paul's volatile nature, it is surprising that he does *not* hurl a blanket anathema against all Jews who resist belief in Jesus as the Messiah. From this he consistently refrains. Here he pronounces God's wrath only upon those who have actively persecuted the Christian movement. We have good reason to believe that these were a small minority within the Judaism of Paul's day. Probably the apostle means to zero in on the priestly officials of Judea (2:14) and their allies. Exactly what he meant by "God's wrath" in this passage remains unclear. His convictional statement that it "has come" may indicate that specific events have recently occurred that render the persecutors "judged" in his eyes.[5]

Galatians 3:10–26 has often been cited as evidence for Paul's total rejection of Judaism.

> For all who rely on works of the law are under a curse; for it is written, "Cursed be every one who does not abide by all things written in the book of the law, and do them." Now it is evident that no man is justified before God by the law; for "He who through faith is righteous shall live"; but the law does not rest on faith, for "He who does them shall live by them." Christ redeemed us from the curse of the law, having become a curse for us—for it is written, "Cursed be every one who hangs on a tree"—that in Christ Jesus the blessing of Abraham might come upon the Gentiles, that we might receive the promise of the Spirit through faith.
>
> To give a human example, brethren: no one annuls even a man's will, or adds to it, once it has been ratified. Now the promises were made to Abraham and to his offspring. It does not say, "And to offsprings," referring to many; but, referring to one, "And to your offspring," which is Christ. This is what I mean: the law, which came four hundred and thirty years afterward, does not annul a covenant previously ratified by God, so as to make the promise void. For if the inheritance is by the law, it is no longer by promise; but God gave it to Abraham by a promise.

Why then the law? It was added because of transgressions, till the offspring should come to whom the promise had been made; and it was ordained by angels through an intermediary. Now an intermediary implies more than one; but God is one.

Is the law then against the promises of God? Certainly not; for if a law had been given which could make alive, then righteousness would indeed be by the law. But the scripture consigned all things to sin, that what was promised to faith in Jesus Christ might be given to those who believe.

Now before faith came, we were confined under the law, kept under restraint until faith should be revealed. So that the law was our custodian until Christ came, that we might be justified by faith. But now that faith has come we are no longer under a custodian; for in Christ Jesus you are all sons of God, through faith. (Gal. 3:10–26)

Here Paul does indeed take a hard line against the Jewish law. Though he concedes that the law ultimately originates with God, he argues that because it came 430 years after the promise to Abraham (and moreover, indirectly, through the angels and Moses), it represents only God's secondary will (3:17–20). Its purpose was never to open up a way of life or righteousness (3:21) but rather to contain and expose sin and to place the guilty under restraint (3:23).

We neither can nor should attempt to make such thoughts palatable to modern Jews, for whom Torah has consistently functioned as a way of life and a path to righteousness. What we *can* do is get behind Paul's words so as to understand how he arrives at such sweeping conclusions. We may begin by noticing that the apostle addresses his words not to all, but only to Gentiles who have already received the Spirit of Jesus apart from Torah observance (Gal. 3:2; 4:6f.). Paul has heard that these Gentile Christians are beginning to combine the way of faith with Torah observance, and he finds this news alarming. As a result of his own conversion, which involved a radical shift from Torah to Christ (see Phil. 3:4ff.), Paul is convinced that one can no longer practice two paths to righteousness simultaneously (Gal. 5:2–5). In his view, believers who attempt to do so will find themselves "severed from Christ" (5:4). Obviously, not all early Christians agreed with Paul on this matter or he would not have felt compelled to write his Galatian letter (see 4:17; 5:12).

The polemic of Gal. 3:10–26 must be read in the light of Paul's attempt to save the Galatians from what he considers to be a perverted gospel (1:7). However, his polemic not only functions to change the minds of the readers; it also serves as a forum for working out an answer to the apostle's own agonizing question: How could God's law and God's Messiah be so different? Paul never doubts that the God of Torah and the God of Jesus Christ are one and the same. Then, however, the only way to understand God's purpose as a single, consistent will, rather than two opposing wills, is to reinterpret Jewish history by showing that God intended the law to function in a much more limited way than most Jews supposed. In Gal. 3:10–26, Paul experiments publicly. His thought remains unfinished and highly emotional because of the crisis he perceives in the Galatian churches. To a large extent, his argument struggles to provide rational reasons for his belief that Christ and Torah observance prove incompatible for attaining righteousness. Even here Paul does not deny the validity of the law and its observance *by Jews*. Nevertheless, the total effect of his reasoning is clearly to devalue the Torah and Judaism. We might call it an "overkill" approach, seized upon in the heat of battle. Earlier it was suggested that Paul modifies his views somewhat in his letter to the Romans, where he has time to work them out more carefully.

A final example of what has been customarily taken to be an uncompromisingly anti-Jewish passage is found in 2 Corinthians:

> Such is the confidence that we have through Christ toward God. Not that we are competent of ourselves to claim anything as coming from us; our competence is from God, who has made us competent to be ministers of a new covenant, not in a written code but in the Spirit; for the written code kills, but the Spirit gives life.
>
> Now if the dispensation of death, carved in letters on stone, came with such splendor that the Israelites could not look at Moses' face because of its brightness, fading as this was, will not the dispensation of the Spirit be attended with greater splendor? For if there was splendor in the dispensation of condemnation, the dispensation of righteousness must far exceed it in splendor. Indeed, in this case, what once had splendor has come to have no splendor at all, because of the splendor that surpasses it.

For if what faded away came with splendor, what is permanent must have much more splendor.

Since we have such a hope, we are very bold, not like Moses, who put a veil over his face so that the Israelites might not see the end of the fading splendor. But their minds were hardened; for to this day, when they read the old covenant, that same veil remains unlifted, because only through Christ is it taken away. Yes, to this day whenever Moses is read a veil lies over their minds; but when a man turns to the Lord the veil is removed. Now the Lord is the Spirit, and where the Spirit of the Lord is, there is freedom. And we all, with unveiled face, beholding the glory of the Lord, are being changed into his likeness from one degree of glory to another; for this comes from the Lord who is the Spirit. (2 Cor. 3:4–18)

Written about the same time as the letter to the Galatians, these words also demonstrate Paul's view that Christians must keep the way of Torah (here called the dispensation of death) separate from and subordinate to the way of Christ (the new covenant or dispensation of righteousness). Like Galatians, this portion of 2 Corinthians is obviously polemical. In the background are Jewish-Christian missionaries (11:22f.) who have introduced themselves to the Corinthians with letters of recommendation from important people (3:1f.). They pronounce Paul's gospel "veiled" (4:3). Paul sets forth his counter opinion so vigorously that we may suspect these Jewish Christians of urging the Corinthians to combine their faith in Christ with Torah observance.

As in Galatians 3, Paul renders ironic homage to Moses and the law (2 Cor. 3:7, 9). In effect, however, his statements function as a judgment that the old way of Torah now manifests "no splendor at all, because of the splendor that surpasses it" (i.e., that of the new covenant). Like Moses' face, the brightness of the old order fades before the dawning light of the new. With vs. 12ff. Paul's argument takes an even sharper turn, for here he introduces the "hardening" motif. Now it is not just a matter of the old giving way to the new. Instead, Paul contends that even prior to the new, when the glory of the ancient covenant remained intact, Israel nevertheless misunderstood its function (3:14ff.). In the apostle's view not even God's chosen people could perceive the purposes behind the law. As in

Galatians, Paul considers that purpose to be limited, that is, to pronounce death and condemnation.

Once again, we Christians must resist well-intentioned but wrong-headed efforts to beautify this passage or remove its barbs. In 2 Corinthians 3, Paul repeats essentially the same ideas he developed in Galatians. He even adds a new one, the "hardening" motif. This indicates that the way of Christ and the way of Torah have become mutually exclusive in his thinking. He does not give this "either-or," even in Romans, although there he sets forth a rather different version of the "two ways" doctrine.

But before we return to Romans, we may profitably reckon with a few details in the 2 Corinthians passage. First, when Paul contrasts the splendor of the old with that of the new, he refrains from citing any concrete examples of the dawning splendor. His argument is logical rather than empirical; in fact, it depends largely on his eschatological assumptions. Thus, he writes, "If there was splendor in the dispensation of condemnation, the dispensation of righteousness must [literally "will"—future tense] far exceed it in splendor" (2 Cor. 3:9). Again, "if what faded away [literally, "what *is fading* away"—present tense] came with splendor, what is permanent must have much more splendor" (3:11). Paul's argument for the superiority of the new presupposes that what one can now see of it represents only the tip of an iceberg. The rest will emerge in the near future. Presently, we know its overwhelming glory only by faith and not by sight (5:7). Paul's attempt to establish the superiority of the new presumes that what is dawning will be permanent. Nothing can resist or supplant the imminent advent of God's Kingdom on earth. Because of this imminence, Paul believes the new is displacing the old. We contemporary Christians will want to ask ourselves how we should interpret Paul's eschatological assumptions now that two thousand years have passed without the demise of Judaism.

A second detail in 2 Corinthians 3 is Paul's use of the hardening motif. While he scarcely pays the Jewish people any compliments in vs. 14ff., neither does he blame them for what he terms their "veiled" minds. The Jews do not harden or veil their minds willfully. Their misunderstanding bears a similarity to what some Roman Catholics call "invincible ignorance." Paul repeats this notion in Rom. 10:2ff., where he says of the Jewish people:

> I bear them witness that they have a zeal for God, but it is not enlightened. For, being ignorant of the righteousness that comes from God, and seeking to establish their own, they did not submit to God's righteousness. (Rom. 10:2–3)

Paul takes care not to ascribe evil intentions to the Jews. He refrains from judging them prideful or hypocritical as a nation. On the contrary, he acknowledges that they pursue the way to righteousness through Torah with honesty and integrity. Paul knew from his own experience that a radical conversion to Christ was required to "enlighten" a person regarding the place and purpose of the Torah (2 Cor. 3:16). Only in those who believe does Christ become the end of the law for righteousness (Rom. 10:4).

ROMANS 9–11: A WATERSHED IN PAUL'S THEOLOGY

Among New Testament scholars, the view has been gaining ground steadily that chapters 9–11 of Romans represent not an extended digression from an otherwise orderly presentation of the Christian faith but a theological climax in the letter. The chief purpose of these chapters is "to define the place for Gentiles in the Church, according to the plan of God."[6] Paul does not write about the place of Gentiles just because he thinks it deserves to be mentioned in his "system." Here, as in his other letters, the concern is practical and situational. The Roman church, which consists of Jewish as well as Gentile Christians, has been experiencing problems of disunity. Paul speaks to those problems in chs. 14 and 15, especially through his appeal to Jewish and Gentile Christians to "welcome one another . . ., as Christ has welcomed you, for the glory of God" (Rom. 15:7). But he does not venture to give this advice until he has laid the theological groundwork for it in chs. 9–11.

Paul's personal problems may be just as relevant for the understanding of Romans as those of his addressees. Ready to set forth for Jerusalem, the apostle feels considerable anxiety about whether he and his Gentile companions will find a happy reception there (15: 25–31). Since Paul clearly desires acceptance by the Jerusalem church, we may suspect that in Romans he is purposely working out his position on the relationship between Christian Jews and Gentiles for his own sake as well as his readers'. In any case, we see him building here what proves to be the last case for his ministry among Gentiles now extant in the New Testament. Perhaps he even intends to lay this defense before Jewish Christians in the Holy City, for as he writes, he finds he must also speak about Jews who do not believe in Christ, that overwhelming majority of the Palestinian population among whom the mother church must live out its mission.

Whether or not the church can continue to exist in Jerusalem depends to a large extent upon its relationship with non-Christian Jews. Perhaps Paul sends his brief for a Gentile ministry to the Romans because he hopes that they can offer him support (letters? emissaries?) in securing a good response from the Jerusalem elders (see 15:30). In any event, the letter to Rome functions as a warm-up for his Jerusalem trip. Through writing it, Paul develops his thought in relative tranquillity, without having to direct it straight at his Jerusalem opponents (see Acts 21:17ff.).

If someone at ease "on the couch" can speak more easily than one who is distracted, and defensive, then the Paul of Romans is probably as close to the "real" Paul as we are going to get. It can hardly be accidental that Paul has more to say about the place of Jews and Judaism in this letter than in any other. His passion seems quite genuine when he writes:

> I am speaking the truth in Christ, I am not lying; my conscience bears me witness in the Holy Spirit, that I have great sorrow and unceasing anguish in my heart. For I could wish that I myself were accursed and cut off from Christ for the sake of my brethren, my kinsmen by race. They are Israelites, and to them belong the sonship, the glory, the covenants, the giving of the law, the worship, and the promises; to them belong the patriarchs, and of their race, according to the flesh, is the Christ. (Rom. 9:1–5)

Paul suffers great torment about the place of the Jewish people within the plan of God as he understands it. At last, he is able to express that pain as pain (in the Spirit!) rather than polemic. He finds it profoundly sad that so few of his coreligionists have come to believe in the person he knows as Messiah. The unbelief of the Jewish majority is no side issue for Paul, for he knows that God's Messiah must be first of all Israel's Messiah. So he struggles to find some satisfactory explanation for the vexing phenomenon before him.

Even in Romans, where Paul enjoys considerable freedom from immediate attacks by his opponents, the answer does not quite come. We shall be disappointed if we expect to discover a final resolution to the numerous tensions we have already noticed in his theology. Yet we do find differences from the earlier letters. For one thing, Paul is now dealing with the status of Jews and Judaism on a more conscious level than ever before. He is letting his loyalty to Israel and his anguish about its present status show through more clearly. Secondly, we find Paul moderating his views on the law from previous letters. In Romans there are carefully worded statements about when the law applies and when it does not (see, e.g., Rom. 10:4). Consistent with this moderation is Paul's claim that, far from overthrowing the law, the righteousness by faith which he advocates will actually uphold it (3:31). Only in Romans do we observe Paul praising the commandments of Torah as "holy and just and good" (7:12). No longer present is the radical suggestion, made earlier in Gal. 3:19f., that from the moment of its origin the law represented only God's secondary will. Instead, Paul discerns an originally spiritual law (Rom. 7:14), weakened by contact with sinful humans and therefore in need of help from God so that the just requirement of its commandments can find satisfaction (7:7–8:4). That help is the righteousness by faith apart from law, shown in the story of Abraham to be God's original intention for all humans (Rom. 4).

A third shift from Paul's earlier letters is his readiness in Romans to let the antinomies of his thought about Israel spring open before his readers with all their offenses to common sense. Indeed, Paul seems almost to flaunt the rough edges of his theologizing. The hardening theme is a case in point. On the one hand, Paul dares to

judge Israel disobedient and therefore responsible for its persistent
unbelief (10:16–21). On the other hand, he interprets this hardening,
which has come upon all but a remnant of the Jewish people, as *God's
doing* (9:18; 11:7–10). When it is so identified, it becomes a facet
of God's redemptive plan by means of which Gentiles gain entry to
the church (11:11–16, 25). From one perspective Israel's disobedience is seen as its own act (11:30); nevertheless, it is God who
consigns Israel (and all others) to disobedience (11:32). This means
that Israel's "trespass" cannot possibly be a stumbling "so as to fall"
(11:11). In the end, Paul comes to understand Jewish disbelief as a
mission of mercy entrusted to Israel by God in the last days (11:
30–32). Paradoxically, Israel fulfills its ancient calling to enlighten the
Gentiles *by means of its own blindness!*

Another antinomy has to do with the Jewish quest for righteousness through Torah. In 10:1ff., Paul compliments Israel for its zeal
while reproaching it for its failure to "submit to God's righteousness." We must set this statement in tension with an earlier passage
where he says that by God's grace the adherents of the law partake
of the promise made to Abraham (4:16). The majority in Israel find
it impossible to accept God's righteousness by faith. But their refusal
turns out to be not so disastrous after all. What the Gentiles receive
through their righteousness by faith, namely, the fulfillment of God's
promised mercy, Israel gains through its original election (11:28–31).
Paul hardly praises Israel's adherence to righteousness through Torah
observance. But neither does he find it a damnable offense. When
he tells the Gentiles in the Roman church: "Brethren, my heart's
desire and prayer to God for them [the Jews] is that they may be
saved" (10:1), he does not fear that Torah-observant Jews who reject
Jesus' Messiahship will suffer eternal separation from God's mercy.
Rather, he means to express a deep wish that they might *presently*
join him and the believing Gentiles in the joys of Jesus' messianic
Kingdom, preeminently the gifts of the Holy Spirit.

Here we must pay close attention to Paul's root-branch imagery,
for it is confusing and capable of many interpretations. The apostle
claims that unbelieving Jews are like branches which have been
"broken off" from a holy root (11:16–17). We might suppose that

this root stands for Israel, the people of God. Then Paul would be asserting that unbelieving Jews have lost their place among God's elect. But he explicitly rejects this conclusion in 11:11, 28–29. Thus, the holy root, into which believing Gentiles have now been grafted (11:17–24), must mean something other than Israel. Probably it refers to the experiential *effects* of the promise-covenant made with Abraham. Through the Spirit, by faith in Christ, Gentiles can now share the resurrection life associated with this promise (4:16–25; 6:1–4; 8:1–4; see also Gal. 3:14). For Paul, this is what it means to be "saved" (Rom. 8:12–27, especially v. 24).

Finally, we may point to a third antinomy in Romans 9–11, that of Israel's opposition to the gospel. On the one hand, Paul can label Jews who deny Jesus' Messiahship "enemies with respect to the gospel" (11:28a). This means that they oppose what Paul takes to be a new act of God at the end of time. On the other hand, the apostle knows that these Jews cannot really be God's enemies, not from an eternal point of view. "As regards election they are beloved [of God] for the sake of their forefathers. For the gifts *(charismata)* and the call of God are irrevocable" (11:28bf.). Strange to tell, Israel's "trespass," its "disobedience," its "enmity" all play a *positive* role in God's plan. For a while, Israel must suffer a division within itself between those who believe and those who do not. But this schism is temporary and providential. The reluctance of Israel's majority to accept God's way of righteousness through Jesus spells opportunity for Gentiles. Soon, however, the allotted number of Gentiles will have entered into God's mercy. Then, part of the world's Gentiles (those who believe) and *all of Israel* will be saved (11:26).

ISRAEL AND CHURCH

Many Christian thinkers have referred to the church as God's "new Israel," often implying thereby that the "old" racial Israel has run its course in the divine economy. Neither the terminology nor the implication represents Paul's thought. Nowhere does Paul refer to the church as Israel.[7] For him, Israel remains the *Jewish* people of God, beloved for the sake of her ancestors. And this people will endure forever. A small part of Israel now belongs to the church. There, Jews can join with Gentiles to glorify God for his mercy. In Gal. 3:28, Paul asserts that this new community contains "neither Jew nor Greek," which is to say that circumcision no longer counts as the exclusive sign of admission to God's favor. But in Romans, Paul shows that he does not really consider all distinctions to have been obliterated. This later, less polemical letter reveals his passion to defend the integrity and dignity of Israel. Thus, just when he wants to highlight the unity between Jews and Gentiles in the church, he quotes Deut. 32:43, a passage that assumes an obvious distance between the two: "Rejoice, O Gentiles, *with his people*" (Rom. 15:10, italics added). Gentiles are God's people too (9:25ff.), but they are not *the people called Israel*, which manifests its unique calling through biological transmission. A distinction between Jew and Gentile continues to exist after all. Even in the new creation, the latter remain younger brothers and sisters, wild olive shoots grafted into the holy root (11:16–24).

Paul's reflections on the place of Israel in Romans 9–11 can hardly function as a "solution" to the split in God's ancient people from the standpoint of contemporary Jewish-Christian dialogue. Obviously, practicing Jews today cannot accept Paul's conclusion that their observance of Torah plays only a secondary role in their relationship with God. Nor will they see their rejection of Jesus' Messiahship as disobedience to God. Paul's presumption that Jews may find salvation only in the Christian sense of receiving the Spirit also remains altogether unacceptable to them. These scandals cannot and should not be removed.

Yet they can be set in perspective. What we must stress today in our study of Paul is the noteworthy fact that his thought moved inexorably toward a hope for reconciliation between Israel and the Christian church. Passages from his letters which run counter to this trend ought to be judged against the background of his mature reflections in Romans. Moreover, while Paul obviously wants his brother and sister Jews to experience a conversion like his, he realizes that for the majority this will simply not be possible. He *might* have concluded from this that the majority of Jews had forfeited their place as God's chosen people and were thus eternally lost. But he never does this. Instead, he strives to interpret Israel's disbelief as a phase in the unfolding of God's merciful will. One conviction he will not give up is that empirical Israel continues to occupy a unique place as God's beloved nation. Despite everything, Jews remain *the* people of promise. Whether they become Christians or not, they will inherit God's mercy. When we consider that Paul struggles to these conclusions when he is encountering substantial opposition from Jews to his missionary work (2 Cor. 11:23–26), we wonder at how conciliatory they sound. For a zealous convert who sees Christian faith and Judaism as incompatible, Paul exhibits remarkable friendliness toward the other side. One does violence to the direction of his thought by placing the major stress on his polemics against Judaism. We stand much closer to the legacy he himself would bequeath if we grant Romans 9–11 a central place of honor in our Pauline canon.

CHAPTER 3

Mark: A Jewish Gospel for Gentiles

THE TRAUMAS OF THE SEVENTH DECADE

In August of the year 66 one of the most tragic wars in Israel's history broke out. Eleazar, a Jew of priestly lineage who was director of the Temple precinct in Jerusalem, announced that daily sacrifices on behalf of the emperor Nero would henceforth cease. Rome correctly interpreted this declaration as an act of rebellion and proceeded, sluggishly at first, to swat the offending fly. But Eleazar was no solitary voice crying in the wilderness. He spoke for a substantial part of the Jewish population in Palestine. His deed mobilized thousands who had suffered long from injustices perpetrated by Roman procurators and their collaborators, the Herodian princes and patrician high priests. Soon throngs of people from nearly every social class and religious sect of Judaism trooped to Jerusalem to enlist in the revolution, especially the young men and the poor, who longed for messianic liberty.

Rome had far more opposition on its hands than it at first suspected. In the end only its best generals and most experienced legions could subdue these determined freedom fighters in one of its tiniest provinces. And then only after four years. The decisive blow fell in August of 70 when Roman troops under Titus succeeded in penetrating the Temple precinct itself. During a skirmish around the main gates a Roman soldier, apparently without orders, hurled a firebrand into the sanctuary. At first, Titus tried to have the flames extinguished. But he soon lost control of his troops, who reveled in the conflagration and proceeded to spread it from one quarter of the sacred compound to another. At day's end, the entire structure lay in ruins. For the first time in six hundred years Jerusalem found itself bereft of a temple for the God of Israel! The effect of this event upon Judaism can hardly be exaggerated. Even today practicing Jews throughout the world mourn the Temple's destruction on the 9th day of the Hebrew month Ab. Losses of physical life and personal liberty during the revolt were staggering. Josephus, a Jewish historian who witnessed the war's climax from a safe distance after defecting to the Roman side, reported that

> the total number of prisoners taken throughout the entire war amounted to ninety-seven thousand, and of those who perished during the siege [of Jerusalem], from first to last, to one million one hundred thousand. (*The Jewish War* VI, 428–32)[1]

Not all Palestinian Jews supported the revolt. As in every revolution, large numbers of the common people suffered and died without declaring allegiance to either side. In addition, one religious subgroup systematically held itself aloof from hostilities for the duration of the war. This was a band of Pharisaic scholars under the leadership of one Johanan ben Zakkai, a disciple of Hillel. The latter, perhaps best known to Christians as the namesake for Jewish student centers on today's college campuses, was Judaism's foremost teacher in the days of Jesus' youth. Of the disciple, Christian scholar W. D. Davies writes:

> Under the influence of the great and gentle Hillel, his teacher, [Johanan] became, like him, in a positive, almost aggressive way, a man of peace. He opposed the policy of armed revolt against Rome from the beginning; and when war finally came his experience of it merely confirmed Johanan in his pacifism. At the appropriate moment, he decided to leave the doomed city [Jerusalem] to found a school in Jamnia where Judaism could preserve its continuity.[2]

Under the leadership of Johanan and his associates, there arose in the small town of Jamnia, thirty-five miles west of Jerusalem, an academy of sages which occupied itself with nothing less than the reconstruction of Judaism. At war's end, the institutions and practices of Israel's religion were in real danger of extinction. No one fostered the illusion that the Temple could soon rise again. The Sadducean high-priestly families, who had exercised great political power until the revolt, were now largely discredited in the eyes of the surviving populace. Indeed, many had perished at the hands of Jewish patriots. The parties of the Zealots and Essenes seem to have suffered virtual annihilation. Of the Pharisees who took part in the revolt, many were slain. But now, at Jamnia, the pacifist scholars of Pharisaism began to gather up the scattered pieces of their religion and shape them into what we have come to call rabbinic Judaism. During the time of Jesus and Paul the term *rabbi,* which literally means "my great one," probably referred to numerous learned and holy men, whether Pharisees or not. At Jamnia, however, the word came to be a title for those recognized by the academy as authentic teachers of Judaism, that is, ordained interpreters of Torah and tradition.

In consolidating the teachings and practices of Judaism to ensure its survival, the Jamnia sages found themselves confronting a difficult question: What was orthodox in their religion and what was not? Thus, the rabbis devoted considerable time to deciding which writings in the Jewish tradition could be accepted as official Scripture. The Torah proper (the Pentateuch), most of the prophets, and many of the psalms had achieved practical canonicity long before this time. But other books, such as Daniel, Ecclesiastes, and the Song of Songs, had not. It was late in the first century before academy scholars could agree upon the thirty-nine books which we today know as the Hebrew Scriptures or Old Testament. Many apocalyptic works were rejected, probably because the rabbis feared that they would stimulate false hopes similar to those which had driven Israel into the disastrous war with Rome.

Sometime in the 80s the sages at Jamnia also felt compelled to draw a sharp line between themselves and the Christian church. We do not yet know all the reasons for this decision. In some cases Christian congregations had already effected a separation by departing from their local synagogues (Acts 19:8–10). This, however, was probably not the practice of most Jewish believers, who constituted the majority among Christians until postwar times. No doubt the growing emphasis in churches on Jesus' divinity caused special offense to the rabbis.

Another stimulus to their decision must have been the tendency among Christians to blur distinctions between Jews and Gentiles. Especially in churches where Gentiles predominated, the ritual laws and traditions of Judaism fell more and more into disuse. The rabbis found this laxity particularly dangerous, for it appeared to threaten the very existence of Jews as a separate, holy people. In the view of the Jamnia sages it was just now, in the postwar chaos, that Jewish traditions needed to be preserved, codified, standardized, and above all, practiced. By celebrating the unity between Jew and Gentile, Christians were moving in exactly the opposite direction. We shall have more to say about the final split between Judaism and Christianity in our examination of the Fourth Gospel (Chapter 6). At present, we simply want to keep aware of trends in Jewish history which may have shaped the attitudes toward Judaism contained in the Synoptic Gospels and Acts.

As Palestinian Judaism moved toward the terrible confrontation with Rome which would restructure its whole religious life, Christians too were experiencing trying times. In the decade between 60 and 70 Christianity lost its three greatest leaders, suffered its first major persecution at the hands of the Roman government, and found itself transformed from a minor sectarian movement composed largely of Jews into a quasi-independent religion with an emerging Gentile majority. Let us look at these upheavals one by one with an eye toward determining what role they might have played in the writing of Mark, Matthew, and Luke-Acts.

The three leaders to whom we refer—all of them Jewish—were James the brother of Jesus, who headed the Jerusalem congregation from the mid-40s until his death in 62, and the apostles Peter and Paul, who suffered martyrdom shortly afterward, probably under Nero.[3] James's death deserves more attention from Christians than it generally receives, for it plays a key role in reconstructing the ecclesiastical history that lies behind the Synoptic Gospels and Acts. The Jerusalem church was by far the most influential Christian community in the early 60s. Under James's leadership it remained solidly Jewish in composition and practice. Nevertheless, according to Josephus, a Jewish council stoned James and some other Jerusalem Christians at the instigation of the newly appointed high priest, Ananus II. Apparently, James was executed on charges of blasphemy (*Jewish Antiquities,* XX. 200). No doubt this execution helped to satisfy conservative elements in Judaism who saw even the strict Jewish-Christian movement as a threat. But it is by no means clear that the majority of Jerusalem Jews felt this way. Josephus reports that some of the more moderate local leaders condemned Ananus' council for acting rashly and lawlessly.

Shortly after James's death leaders in the church of Jerusalem concluded that the community could no longer live in safety with its neighbors and ordered a migration to the small Hellenistic city of Pella some sixty air miles to the northeast in present-day Jordan (Eusebius, *Ecclesiastical History* 3. 5. 2f.). Pella lay outside the high priest's official jurisdiction. This move was probably completed by the war's onset in 66, though some believers must have remained behind in Judea, perhaps even in Jerusalem. No extant Jewish or Christian source indicates that members of the church chose sides in the hostilities or suffered atrocities because of them. It is probable that Christians took a pacifist position.

In prewar Rome, however, the situation was different. Current historians of the ancient world tend to view the persecution of Christians there under Nero as a scapegoat operation. Someone had to take the blame for the city's burning in 64, and the church served as a ready candidate. It had already acquired a certain public reputation for despising the civil religion of the Empire. Nero's act was no systematic attempt to destroy the church everywhere. Nor did he justify it on the legal grounds that Christians had offended his imperial majesty by refusing to perform certain patriotic rituals. The whole persecution seems to have been a pragmatic move in a crisis. On Nero's order, soldiers and private citizens hunted out known Christians and, having accused them before the judiciary, handed them over for burning, crucifixion, or ripping apart by wild animals. The purpose was to satisfy the inhabitants of the city who were enraged by the destruction of their homes.

Jews did not suffer in this mob action unless, like Peter, they were also known to be Christians. This means that even before 70 the Roman government proved capable of distinguishing between the two groups. It seems most unlikely, therefore, that the pro-Jewish attitudes we shall discover in the Gospels and Acts represent attempts to elicit from government authorities those special privileges and safeguards which accrued to Judaism in the Greco-Roman world[4] on grounds that Christians were essentially Jewish. Had church leaders wanted to engage in such a strategy, they could probably have foreseen that it would backfire. In the generation following the 66–70 war Gentiles typically harbored great hate against the "rebellious Jews."[5] The massive triumphal arch of Titus, which stands to this day in the forum at Rome, with its bas-relief of the Temple's looting, shows what elaborate efforts were made to perpetuate the subjugation of the Jews in the minds of the general public.

A third upheaval experienced by the Christian church, its shift in status from a Jewish sect to a mixed movement with increasing Gentile leadership, was probably the most transformative of all. Paul's mission to Gentiles in the 40s and 50s had succeeded, though on a relatively small scale. In the late 50s he himself speculated that the open-door policy toward Gentiles which he was advocating would not last much longer. Very soon, he sensed, Christ would return from heaven to complete the Gentile harvest and save "all Israel" (Rom. 11:25–32; 13:10ff.). As we have noted in the previous chapter, Paul continued to regard Jewish Christians, particularly those at Jerusalem, at first among equals in the church. From his point of view, they deserved honor and material support from their younger brothers and sisters, the Gentile Christians (Rom. 15:16, 26–27).

Events did not unfold just the way Paul envisioned them. By war's end, Christ had not yet returned and the influence of the Jerusalem church on world Christianity had diminished to practically nil. No creative theologies or great acts of faith issued forth from Pella. No Jewish-Christian missionaries of the stature of Peter or Paul visited the churches in Asia Minor and Europe to remind them of their continuing link with Israel. Instead, Rome, with its martyrs and gift for teaching, replaced Jerusalem as the church most honored by believers. And Roman Christians were predominantly Gentile. As we have noted, Judaism itself suffered decline from the late 60s to the middle 70s and thus offered no vigorous competition to the Christian mission. The script for the rest of the century had been written: Christianity would flourish as a chiefly *Gentile* phenomenon. All of this means that in approaching the Synoptic Gospels and Acts, we shall do well to evaluate the attitudes toward Judaism we find there *in the light of world-historical forces impinging upon synagogue and church.* Anything less will result in a misreading of the text.

THE GOOD NEWS ACCORDING TO MARK

Mark's use of Greek indicates that he was Semitic in background —possibly Jewish. The Semitic flavor of his word choice, grammar, and sentence structure would have been apparent to his first readers, wherever they may have resided. For his part, Mark seems to have envisioned these readers as Greco-Roman Gentiles, for he takes care to translate for them most of the Hebrew or Aramaic words he uses (Mk. 3:17; 5:41; 7:11, 34; 10:46; 15:34).[6] At the same time, he explains Jewish customs with which he thinks his addressees may be unfamiliar (7:3–4).[7]

In all likelihood, Mark thought of his primary readers as practicing Christians. The purpose of his Gospel is not to convert but to instruct and encourage. This comes out especially in his strong emphasis upon the necessity and benefits of following Jesus as suffering servant (8:34–38; 10:28–31, 35–45; 13:3–13). It sounds very much as though Mark is writing to Christians who have suffered—or are about to suffer. Who are these people? We cannot be sure, since they are nowhere named in the Gospel. The Christians at Rome, known to the whole church after 64 as martyrs and fugitives under Nero, are strong candidates.

Much depends on when we date the Gospel. The majority of scholars today argue for a time around 70 on grounds that the thirteenth chapter of Mark reflects the Jewish war of 66–70 as current event or recent history. This chapter takes the form of an extended prophecy by Jesus concerning the Temple's destruction and the end of the present world order, with his own return from heaven as Son of Man climaxing the process. It is hard to tell which parts of this prophecy come directly from Jesus and which parts represent elaborations on his original words by the early church or Mark.

Nothing in the chapter requires us to date the present form of the prophecy *after* Jerusalem's demise in 70. On the contrary, there is much that suggests a time prior to 70. For example, the writer gives no hint that the Temple will perish *in flames* (13:1–2). Moreover, the chief event that signals the beginning of the end time is some kind of desecration (as in 2 Thess. 2:3–4), not a destruction (Mk. 13:14). Finally, what is to take place will unfold in such a way that Christians still living in Judea will have time to flee from it (13:14–20).[8] Certainty is unattainable on these matters, but Mark 13 looks very much like a prophecy of Jesus modified to fit the late 60s, when Roman troops were closing in on Jerusalem and great chaos seemed imminent.

Why does Mark devote so much attention to these current events and even (so it appears) try to link them with the end of the present world order (13:14–27)? Mark himself clearly thought that Jesus soon would return from heaven (9:1; 13:30). His impatient readers had probably suffered recent persecution under Nero and would naturally wish to interpret the events in Palestine as an impending reversal of empirical power that would vindicate their suffering. But Mark's chief counsel seems to be that Jesus' return will *not* coincide with the climax of the Jewish-Roman war. Instead, a process of world disintegration must take place (13:6–13), some of it "after that [wartime] tribulation" (13:24–27). In God's providence, sufficient time will be given for the gospel to be "preached to all nations" (13:10). Through Jesus' prophecy, Mark's message to his Gentile readers is that they must endure, watch, and serve (13:13, 32–37; 10:42–45). The end will take longer than they think and in any case cannot be so clearly discerned as to plot its exact arrival (13:32–33). Mark's Gospel is a "cool" apocalypse. To be sure, Christ's return will come soon, but its nearness should stimulate true disciples to activity (13:34–36), not satisfied resignation. More suffering will follow, but this too has its purpose in God's plan of salvation.

We must pause here to take note of what Mark is *not* doing. He is clearly not rejoicing in the devastation about to befall Judea. He takes no pleasure in the suffering of the Jewish people, nor does he urge his Gentile readers to do so. Evidence that Mark sees the mounting tribulation in Judea as a judgment upon Jews for having rejected and crucified Jesus is altogether lacking. This is remarkable because such a conclusion could have been drawn quite easily by Christian writers in the late 60s. But Mark is no hater of Jews. His harsh critiques of Jewish leaders, which we shall examine in a moment, cannot be taken as a curse upon the people as a whole or as a repudiation of their unique election by God.[9]

THE NATURE OF MARK'S POLEMIC

Mark's Gospel has received some bad press recently with regard to its attitude toward Jews. Historian Michael Grant refers to "Mark's attacks on the Jews," characterizing them as "numerous and savage."[10] Rosemary Ruether, a Christian theologian, detects in Mark's version of the parable of the vineyard (12:1–12) a prejudice that "the Jews have always killed the prophets."[11] Let us examine the passages cited by these two critics and then move on to others which might be taken as anti-Judaistic in the sense that they appear to undercut the structure of Jewish belief and practice.

Grant lists as typical of "Mark's attack on the Jews 2:6, 16; 3:16 [sic; probably 3:6 is meant]; 14:55–64; and 15:10."[12] These verses refer to conflicts between Jesus and certain Jewish leaders. In 2:6 the scribes question Jesus' right to forgive sins. According to 2:16 the "scribes of the Pharisees" express displeasure over Jesus' practice of eating with tax collectors and sinners. The long passage from ch. 14 is a narration of Jesus' trial that begins with the words: "Now the chief priests and the whole council sought testimony against Jesus to put him to death." In 15:10 we learn that in Mark's view Pilate "perceived that it was out of envy that the chief priests had delivered [Jesus] up."

It is certainly true that Mark sees Jesus engaged in battles with

Jewish authorities, *some* of which led finally to his death. But the key word is *some*, for according to the Gospel narrative, only a few conflicts actually result in a decision to seek Jesus' death. It follows that for Mark many leaders, probably the great majority, had no desire to execute Jesus. Mark witnesses to this truth indirectly. Most of the actual confrontations he narrates take place between Jesus and the Pharisees or the scribes (Bible scholars) of the Pharisees (2:15–28; 3:1–6; 7:1–13; 8:11–13; 10:2–12; 12:13–17).[13] In every case these disputes have to do with differences between Jesus and the Pharisees over Torah interpretation or observance. Such arguments were common in first-century Judaism and hardly ever became grounds for criminal trials before Roman officials. (See Chapter 1.) In one instance Mark does note that a group of Pharisees who had witnessed a healing by Jesus on the Sabbath "held counsel with the Herodians against him, how to destroy him" (3:6). But later in the Marcan story these plotting Pharisees drop from view. Possibly they are referred to in 12:13, where Mark records that "they [the chief priests and scribes and elders] sent to him some of the Pharisees and some of the Herodians, to entrap him in his talk." But the most we can deduce from this evidence is that in Mark's view *some* Pharisees, namely, those under the thumb of the high priests, sought Jesus' undoing. In the passages where Jesus himself is shown predicting his death, Pharisees are never mentioned as the agents (see 8:31; 9:31; 10:33f.).

To be sure, Mark frequently implicates the chief priests and the elders in Jesus' execution (8:31; 10:33; 11:18; 11:27ff.; 14:1f.; 14:10; 14:43, 53–65; 15:1–3, 10–13, 31). These people held the chief political authority among Jews in Palestine up to 70. Many of them were Hellenistically inclined patricians, far removed from the everyday lives of ordinary Jews. Recent investigations by both Jewish and Christian scholars have issued in the conclusion that some combination of prominent priests, scholars, and laymen did play a role in handing Jesus over to Pilate. But the exact circumstances remain unclear.[14] In actual number, these patrician leaders were far exceeded by Pharisees, i.e., pious middle-class laymen (and lesser priests) who cared little for power politics. An even larger group of common folk, the *'am ha'aretz*, or "people of the land," constituted the majority of Jews living in Palestine during Jesus' time and probably belonged to no organized religious party at all. Mark pictures them as hearing Jesus "gladly" (12:37). In his view, it must have been only a small fraction of this sympathetic crowd, namely, those incited by the chief priests, who turned against Jesus and demanded his crucifixion before Pilate (14:11–15). As for Mark's assertion that "the whole council sought testimony against Jesus to put him to death" (14:55), this may be understood as an exaggeration analogous to his prior observation that "all the country of Judea and all the people of Jerusalem" came out to confess their sins before John the Baptist (1:5). Mark corrects his own overstatement about Jewish leadership when he tells us that Joseph of Arimathea, "a respected member of the council," gave up his own tomb to bury Jesus (15:42–45).

We see then that the charge against Mark that he attacks "the Jews" frequently and savagely must be challenged as misleading, especially if one presumes to base it on the texts we have examined so far. Mark takes a position against *some* Jewish leaders. His view of "the Jews" in general is quite complex.

But what of the allegation by Professor Ruether that Mark uses the parable of the vineyard (12:1–12) to impress upon his Gentile readers that "the Jews have always killed the prophets"? This too turns out to be a misreading of the text. Let us review the story line of this parable. A group of tenants occupying a vineyard withhold the harvest from its owner. They beat some of his emissaries, kill others, and finally murder even his "beloved son" whom he has sent in a final attempt to retrieve his grapes (12:7–8). The parable closes with these words:

> What will the owner of the vineyard do? He will come and destroy the tenants, and give the vineyard to others. Have you not read this scripture:
> "The very stone which the builders rejected
> has become the head of the corner;
> this was the Lord's doing,
> and it is marvelous in our eyes"? (Mk. 12:9–11)

In its Marcan version, which is already an allegorical development from Jesus' original story, this parable almost certainly refers to a rejection of the Messiah and God's coming judgment upon his rejectors. But who are these guilty ones? The setting of the parable provided by Mark makes it quite clear. The intended targets of the story, in his view, are "the chief priests and the scribes and the elders" (11:27; 12:1, 12). This parable represents no condemnation of the Jewish people as a whole—they are the vineyard in the story. It condemns Jewish leaders, but only *insofar as they have rejected God's envoys*. Israel's ancient prophets had already leveled similar charges against many kings and religious functionaries in their day. Through the parable, Mark is predicting to his readers that part of Israel's present leadership will meet with destruction and be replaced by "others," chief among them Jesus himself. The first element of this prophecy finds a type of fulfillment in the rise to power of the rabbinic academy at Jamnia after 70. The second element comes to fruition *for Christians* in the belief that the resurrected Jesus reigns as Lord over all.

Let us proceed now to examine other Marcan passages that a modern reader might be tempted to take as anti-Judaistic. Some Christians, for example, wrongly read 2:21–22 as a declaration by Jesus (and Mark) of Judaism's obsolescence. Here Jesus is reported as saying:

> No one sews a piece of unshrunk cloth on an old garment; if he does, the patch tears away from it, the new from the old, and a worse tear is made. And no one puts new wine into old wineskins; if he does, the wine will burst the skins, and the wine is lost, and so are the skins; but new wine is for fresh skins. (Mk. 2:21–22)

Whatever these words meant when Jesus originally spoke them (or something comparable), Mark does not interpret them as a blanket rejection of Judaism. The point at issue in this passage is limited to whether Jesus' disciples should fast (see 2:18ff.). The Pharisees say yes. Jesus, however, endorses the continuous meal celebrations of his followers on the grounds that "as long as they have the bridegroom with them, they cannot fast" (2:19). That is, the disciples cannot help rejoicing at table, especially when Jesus brings healing to sinners (2:15–17). Jesus' advent represents a new chapter in Judaism which cannot be properly contained by the contemporary Pharisaic under-standing of fasting.[15] Here the Marcan Jesus does challenge a basic Pharisaic conviction, namely, that the old teachings can always stretch, by means of interpretation, to accommodate a new situation. For the present, says Mark's Jesus, tradition is simply incapable of bending itself around his ministry so as to enclose and categorize it. Rather, the ancient wisdom must be set aside temporarily (2:20) so as to preserve the integrity of both old and new. According to Acts, the moderate Pharisee Gamaliel advocated a similar policy before the Jerusalem council as it deliberated over how to deal with the young church in its midst:

> Men of Israel, take care what you do with these men [the apostles]. . . . I tell you, keep away from these men and let them alone; for if this plan or this undertaking is of men, it will fail; but if it is of God, you will not be able to overthrow them. You might even be found opposing God! (Acts 5:35, 38–39)

Mark's version of the sayings by Jesus concerning cloth and wineskins hardly represents an intention to pronounce judgment upon all Jew-ish tradition, or even upon all Pharisaic tradition. In Mk. 2:20 the Evangelist actually authorizes fasting for his readers, who know that Jesus is no longer present with them physically.

On another occasion, Jesus appears to set his teaching not only in opposition to tradition but over against the very Scriptures them-selves (Mk. 10:2–12). The story depicts a controversy with some Pharisees over the lawfulness of divorce, and Jesus takes a hard line. He dismisses the permission granted in Deut. 24:1, 3 to divorce one's wife at will as a commandment written by Moses for Israel's "hard-ness of heart" (10:5). Quoting from Gen. 2:24; 5:2, Jesus contends that God's original will "from the beginning of creation" was that married couples ought never to separate. "What therefore God has joined together, let not man put asunder" (10:9). The careful reader will note that Mark here shows Jesus quoting one passage of the Pentateuch against another: Moses versus Moses. The primal com-mandment from Genesis is pronounced more authoritative than the later pragmatic one. In essence, this dispute between Jesus and the

Pharisees boils down to a conflict between two sets of interpretive principles. Both sides accept the Hebrew Scriptures as God's will. Mark has no desire to deny this basic tenet of Judaism.

Mark 4:10–12 is a harder case. Here Jesus is asked by the disciples to explain his reasons for using parables. Jesus replies:

> To you has been given the secret of the kingdom of God, but for those outside everything is in parables; so that they may indeed see but not perceive, and may indeed hear but not understand; lest they should turn again, and be forgiven. (Mk. 4:11–12)

In this passage it looks as if the Marcan Jesus wishes to deceive all hearers but his disciples "lest they . . . be forgiven." A horrendous mission, to be sure! But we need to look beneath the surface of this offense. The clause starting with "so that" and ending with "forgiven" is a direct quotation from Is. 6:9–10. The ancient prophet hears God saying that the very message he is to proclaim to Israel will function as a divine hardening.

It is possible that Jesus actually quoted this Old Testament passage in a burst of frustration; or perhaps he meant it ironically. But such explanations are not explicit in the Synoptic texts. It is more plausible to suppose that a prophet of the early church or Mark himself added the words from Isaiah to explain why Jesus' ministry had not met with greater success among Jews. It would then be close to Paul's paradoxical view of Israel's temporary hardening expressed in Rom. 11:11–32. For Paul, it is God himself who produces "blindness" among Jews for a season so as to open a door of faith for Gentiles. Interestingly, the Matthean and Lucan versions of Mk. 4:10–12 tend to soften the first Evangelist's sharp point inasmuch as they do not depict an intention on Jesus' part to withhold forgiveness (see Mt. 13:11–15; Lk. 8:9–10). The Marcan version, harsh to the point of cruelty, ought not to be taken as Jesus' or Mark's typical attitude toward Jews for all time. Mark knew that after the resurrection many Jews did come to understand Jesus' parables and experience God's forgiveness through his message.

A passage near the end of Mark's Gospel may appear to communicate a rejection of Jewish religion *in toto*. We refer to the dramatic announcement in the passion story that just as Jesus died "the curtain of the temple was torn in two, from top to bottom" (Mk. 15:38). One might easily conclude that Mark intends this verse to declare Judaism's bankruptcy. But it need not mean that, and there is strong evidence to suggest that Mark wishes it to serve another purpose. He alone, of all the Evangelists, sandwiches this verse in between the terse statement that "Jesus . . . breathed his last" (15:37) and a cameo report of one witness's response to his death:

> And when the centurion, who stood facing him, saw that he thus breathed his last, he said, "Truly this man was the [or "a"] Son of God!" (Mk. 15:39)

Since the Gentile soldier was looking at Jesus' face, he could have known nothing about the tearing of the Temple curtain which occurred simultaneously almost half a mile away. This latter information, which disturbs the logical flow from v. 37 to v. 39, is a parable for Mark's readers. Apparently, the Evangelist uses it to inform his addressees that through Jesus' death Judaism has "opened up" for them.[16] The Divine Presence dwelling in Judaism's Holy of Holies now reveals itself to Gentiles (symbolized by the centurion) in the cross. At this precise moment, the Temple does indeed become "a house of prayer for all the nations" (11:17), just as God originally intended it to be. First Jesus dies. Then the sanctuary curtain tears. And only then does the soldier "see" Jesus as Son of God. The *veil before his eyes* parts.

This exposure of the Temple chamber does not mean that Judaism has disintegrated, but rather that its treasures will henceforth extend to all people through the sacrificial death of Jesus. For Mark, the incident of the torn Temple curtain is the proleptic beginning of the Gentile mission. The open Temple will allow Gentiles to approach and worship in the very dwelling of God on Mt. Zion, just as Jewish tradition had predicted they would do in the messianic age (Is. 2:1–4; 60:1–3; Mic. 4:1–7; Zech. 14:8–19; Tob. 13:11–13; Ps. of Sol. 17: 30–31). To be sure, Mark does render a final judgment in his Gospel against the current Temple. Mark's Jesus clearly foretells its destruction (13:1–2), despite its cleansing by his act and teaching (see

11:15–13:2). Yet there is no evidence that the Evangelist understands Jesus' prophecy to be a claim that the church of his day has *replaced* the Temple as God's dwelling place. More likely Mark considers the Temple's approaching demise a judgment upon its failure, in his eyes, to follow out its destiny as house of prayer for all nations after its symbolic "opening" at Jesus' death. Such a judgment hardly constitutes the condemnation of Judaism as such.[17]

Up to this point in our study Mark refrains from crossing over the line that distinguishes family disputes from anti-Judaism. While he quarrels with Judaism through his narration of Jesus' ministry, this looks like a criticism from within. Overall, the Jesus of his Gospel remains fundamentally Jewish in both the ethnic and the religious sense. Yet there is one major exception to this general rule. According to 7:14–23, the Marcan Jesus essentially rejects the whole Jewish system of ritual purity with regard to foods, that is, the kosher laws. Having attributed to Jesus the statement that "there is nothing outside a man which by going into him can defile him" (7:15), Mark addresses his readers with the parenthetical remark: "Thus he declared all foods clean" (7:19). If Mark's interpretation is correct, Jesus here places himself in direct opposition to the very words of Scripture, for the kosher food laws were never just a matter of oral tradition. They occur throughout the book of Leviticus (Lev. 7:22ff.; 11:1–46; 17:10ff.) and were accepted as binding by all branches of Judaism at the time of Jesus. There is no passage from the Hebrew Scriptures which one might quote against them.

During his ministry the historical Jesus probably never intended to declare all foods ritually clean. According to Acts 10:1–16, this view first surfaces sometime after the resurrection when Peter sees a vision of "all kinds of animals and reptiles and birds of the air" and hears a heavenly voice commanding him to "kill and eat" (Acts 10:12–13). Even then, Luke's Peter resists the anti-kosher meaning of his vision, preferring instead to understand it as a command that he "should not call any *man* common or unclean" (10:28, italics added). Long after Peter's vision Jewish Christians continued to practice the laws of *kashruth* (Acts 15:19–21, 28–29; 21:17–20). In fact, the Matthean parallel to Mark's story omits both of the key Marcan interpretations

(7:15 and 19). According to Matthew, this whole dispute between Jesus and the Pharisees centered on whether food eaten with unwashed hands would defile a person. It had nothing to do with whether the kosher laws themselves were now abrogated (see Mt. 15:11–20). Luke dispenses with the story altogether.

In 7:14–23, if nowhere else, Mark becomes anti-Judaistic. That is, he undercuts a fundamental practice of Judaism. Since this is not his characteristic line, we must ask why he takes it here. Mark's interpretation probably stems from a confusion experienced by the church of his day regarding the status of the kosher food laws. In the course of his mission to Asia Minor and Europe, Paul had come to the conclusion that Gentiles did not need to observe these laws. A church council in Jerusalem about 48 modified this position by decreeing that in Antioch, Syria, and Cilicia, where the churches contained many Jews, Gentile Christians should abstain from food sacrificed to idols, from blood, and from strangled animals (Acts 15:23, 29). It is unlikely that Paul ever considered this rule binding on the Gentile congregations to which he wrote (see 1 Cor. 8; 10:23–33; Rom. 14). He himself, though self-consciously Jewish, seems to have obeyed the kosher laws only selectively (1 Cor. 9:9–23; Gal. 2:11–14). Mark may have derived his understanding of *kashruth* from Paul (compare Mk. 7:19 with Rom. 14:14). Perhaps he also knew of Peter's vision and interpreted it more radically than the Lucan Peter did. By the time Mark wrote in the late 60s Jerusalem had suffered eclipse as the central Christian church, and Gentile practices were beginning to prevail as the norm. Mark's reading of a Gentile viewpoint back into the ministry of Jesus is almost certainly an error. However, in the light of his Gospel as a whole, we would do him an injustice by labeling it a willful attempt to undermine Judaism. Perhaps it was an inevitable development, given the historical situation in his church.

ISRAEL'S PRIMACY
IN THE MINISTRY OF MARK'S JESUS

Concluding our study of Mark's attitudes toward Judaism, we shall examine two passages that point up his loyalty to Israel. The first is an extraordinary pericope which he alone preserves. In 12:28–34 Mark tempers his usual criticism of Israel's leaders by telling a story about Jesus' high praise for a scribe, i.e., a scholar of the Hebrew Scriptures. It will serve our interests to quote the entire passage:

> And one of the scribes came up and heard them [Jesus and the Sadducees] disputing with one another, and seeing that he answered them well, asked him, "Which commandment is the first of all?" Jesus answered, "The first is 'Hear, O Israel: The Lord our God, the Lord is one; and you shall love the Lord your God with all your heart, and with all your soul, and with all your mind, and with all your strength.' The second is this, 'You shall love your neighbor as yourself.' There is no other commandment greater than these." And the scribe said to him, "You are right, Teacher; you have truly said that he is one, and there is no other but he; and to love him with all the heart, and with all the understanding, and with all the strength, and to love one's neighbor as oneself, is much more than all whole burnt offerings and sacrifices." And when Jesus saw that he answered wisely, he said to him, "You are not far from the kingdom of God." (Mk. 12:28–34)

Though Matthew and Luke record parallel versions of Jesus' words on the Great Commandment, only Mark includes the section beginning with "And the scribe said to him . . . ." In Mark's version of the pericope Jesus sees that the scribe answers "wisely" and commends him by telling him that he is "not far from the kingdom of God." We must take care not to interpret these words as mere condescension on the part of Mark's Jesus. The Evangelist clearly understands them as a genuine compliment. Throughout his Gospel no one, with the possible exception of Jesus himself, lives *in* the Kingdom of God prior to its final coming (compare 9:1, 47; 10:15, 23–31; 11:10; 14:25). Jesus' disciples have learned something of the Kingdom's mysteries (4:11), though they nearly always behave as if they had not (6:52; 8:32f.; 9:9–10, 28–37; 10:13, 26, 32, 42ff., etc.). Joseph of Arimathea longs for the coming of the Kingdom (15:43). But only our scribe, who is not even a follower of Jesus, is said to be *near* it. This fact becomes even more striking when we note that the basis for Jesus' compliment (the scribe's commentary on his words) must be considered altogether Jewish in the most classical sense. In fact, the scribe's answer is essentially a chain of quotations from and allusions to the Hebrew Scriptures (Deut. 4:35; 6:4f.; Is. 45:21; Lev. 19:18; 1 Sam. 15:22; Hos. 6:6). We find nothing distinctively Christian or Christological about it since it never attributes messianic authority to Jesus. Simply put, this Marcan passage shows Jesus praising a Jewish scholar for capsulizing the best of Judaism. No Pharisee in the time of Jesus or Mark would have disagreed with a word of the scribe's answer.

The final passage we shall consider occurs in the midst of Mark's Last Supper story. In the best Greek texts, Mk. 14:23–24 reads: "And [Jesus] took a cup, and when he had given thanks he gave it to them, and they all drank of it. And he said to them, 'This is my blood of the covenant, which is poured out for many.' " Most of us Christians have grown used to hearing these so-called "words of institution" in their Pauline or Lucan form, where Jesus calls the cup "the *new* covenant in my blood" (1 Cor. 11:25; Lk. 22:20; italics added). But one firm principle of modern textual scholarship, which attempts to reconstruct the earliest text of a given passage, is this: other things being equal, the "more difficult" of two variant readings will probably be the more genuine. In this case the more difficult text, for ancient as well as contemporary Christians, is certainly the Marcan one. Although Paul's version arose quite early, probably to highlight the radicality of the Christian movement, Mark's text must stand closer to what Jesus really said. It demonstrates Mark's concern to show Jesus as a Jew who considered his final work to be a mission within and on behalf of Israel. *The* covenant is of course the ancient covenant which God made first with Abraham and then reaffirmed at Sinai with the Israelites whom Moses had led out of Egypt. The blood of Mark's Jesus renews *this* covenant. Although Jesus' death opens up God's ancient election to Gentiles (Mk. 15: 37–39), it challenges in no way the permanent validity of that election for the Jewish people.

MARK AND THE GENTILES

Before gathering our conclusions about Mark's views on Judaism, we need to look at his attitudes toward Gentiles. The first thing that strikes us is that for an Evangelist who writes to and in support of Gentiles, Mark says surprisingly little about them. Prior to the passion narrative, only two Gentiles appear in his Gospel. The first, a Gerasene demoniac who is healed by Jesus, wants to express his gratitude by joining his benefactor's band of disciples. But Jesus rejects his offer with the words, "Go home to your friends, and tell them how much the Lord has done for you." (See Mk. 5:1–20.) The second Gentile in Mark's Gospel is the so-called Syrophoenician woman, who pleads with Jesus to exorcise her demon-tormented daughter. Mark narrates this event as follows:

> And [Jesus] said to her, "Let the children [i.e., Jews] first be fed, for it is not right to take the children's bread and throw it to the dogs." But she answered him, "Yes, Lord; yet even the dogs under the table eat the children's crumbs." And he said to her, "For this saying you may go your way; the demon has left your daughter." And she went home, and found the child lying in bed, and the demon gone. (Mk. 7:27–30)

As Mark sees it, the healings bestowed upon these two Gentiles constitute exceptions to the general rule that Jesus came first of all to serve Israel. In contrast to Matthew and Luke, Mark tells no story about the Roman centurion who beseeches Jesus to heal his servant with a word and receives the accolade: "Not even in Israel have I found such faith" (Mt. 8:10//Lk. 7:9). Mark withholds all praise from *Roman* Gentiles until he has introduced his own centurion in 15:39. And even this man does little more than accept an insight granted to him by God. He is largely a symbolic figure and Mark does not commend him for great faith (contrast the heroic belief of a Jewish father in Mk. 9:23–24).

It has been alleged that "the Gospels elaborately play down the responsibility of the Romans" in the death of Jesus.[18] But this view does not apply well to Mark, for he clearly holds Pontius Pilate accountable for a criminal act. The highest compliment Mark pays the Roman procurator is to record his awareness "that it was out of envy that the chief priests had delivered [Jesus] up" (15:10). But this hardly absolves him of responsibility. Never do we hear from Mark that Pilate washed his hands before the Jewish crowd to demonstrate his innocence of Jesus' blood (Mt. 27:24). Nor does Mark tell us that Pilate's wife warned him against condemning "that righteous man [Jesus]" (Mt. 27:19). Luke has Pilate protesting to the crowd: "I have found in [Jesus] no crime deserving death" (Lk. 23:22). Mark's story contains no hint that the procurator ever reached such a conclusion. Instead, he simply notes that "Pilate, wishing to satisfy the crowd, released for them Barabbas; and having scourged Jesus, he delivered him to be crucified" (Mk. 15:15). This is no elaborate cover-up of Roman responsibility. As far as Mark is concerned, Pilate's resistance to crowd pressure must be judged absolutely minimal. If Jesus' innocence were taken as factual, a modern jury would probably hear Mark's account as evidence that the procurator had conspired to bring about his prisoner's death.

To Mark's sketch of Pilate we may add his narration of the brutal treatment suffered by Jesus at the hands of Roman soldiers (15: 16–20; omitted by Luke), as well as the vignettes of Roman cruelty in the impressment of Simon of Cyrene to carry the cross (15:21) and the game of dice for Jesus' garments at the foot of the cross (15:24). We must conclude that Mark lays a heavy load of guilt upon the Roman government. And this, of course, fits precisely with his purpose: to convince his readers that they must follow in Jesus' footsteps as (apparent) victims of the Empire's mindless wrath. For Mark, acutely conscious of the recent persecution under Nero, it is Roman leadership as well as Jewish leadership that ravages the righteous (see 10:33–34; 13:9, 13).

CONCLUSION

When we Christians interpret Mark for our time, particularly in dialogue with Jews, we need not strive to prove that he holds all the "right" attitudes toward Judaism, whatever these may be. Like the rest of the New Testament authors, Mark is a fallible human being subject to the contingencies of his own history. His work must always stand open to criticism by Jews and others who may feel that he has done them an injustice. One might say, for example, that Mark opens a great breach between Judaism and Christianity when he reads the abrogation of the kosher laws into Jesus' ministry. Not even Paul did that.

On the other hand, neither Jews nor Christians need burden themselves and one another with the simplistic view that "the Gospels" are essentially anti-Judaistic or even anti-Semitic.[19] With Mark much of the evidence points in just the opposite direction. Precisely for Gentiles, Mark underscores the Jewishness of Jesus and his mission. He does this not because he perceives some incipient anti-Semitism in his readers but simply because, for him, it is the way one must tell the story of Jesus.

Let us pause for a moment to reflect on the importance of these conclusions. Most scholars today believe that Mark is the earliest Gospel. This means that the prototype for the other three canonical Gospels, written to Gentiles at a time when Judaism's stock was sinking throughout the Empire, assumes a positive (if difficult) connection between empirical Israel and the Christian movement. Mark apparently thinks that his Gentile readers will have no trouble finding themselves in the Jewish story he has written for them—even before his centurion appears in 15:39. Mark's Jewishness raises at least two important questions for us. First, should we modern interpreters of the New Testament evaluate the later Gospels in Mark's light? Second, should we not ponder whether the Israel-church connection presumed by him continues even to this day?

CHAPTER 4

Matthew:
A Claim on Israel's Leadership

MATTHEW'S JEWISH-CHRISTIAN COMMUNITY

In contrast to Mark, Matthew seldom explains either Hebrew expressions or Jewish customs to his readers (see, e.g., Mt. 5:22; 6:24; 23:5, 24, 27; 27:6; and compare Mt. 15:2 with Mk. 7:2f.). Moreover, he uses certain literary/theological conventions distinctive to scholarly circles in first-century Judaism and expects his readers to understand.[1] These data make it quite likely that Matthew thinks of his readers as Greek-speaking Jewish Christians who are acquainted with the nuances of Palestinian Judaism. To elaborate on just one example, Matthew frequently employs so-called formula quotations. These are editorial comments that interpret an event in the life of Jesus by means of prophecies found in the Jewish Scriptures. The texts cited usually follow upon words such as: "All this took place to fulfil what the Lord had spoken by the prophet . . ." (Mt. 1:22f.; see also 2:6f., 15, 17f., 23; 4:14–16; 8:17; 12:17–21; 13:35; 21:4f.; 27:9f.). Matthew generally quotes the Scripture in its Septuagint (LXX) form, familiar to all Greek-speaking Jews in the first century. But in the formula quotations, where he tips his theologian's hand, he often introduces a Biblical quotation more akin to the Hebrew text than to that found in the LXX.[2] Matthew must have expected his readers to notice these refinements and view them approvingly as a mark of his expertise in Scripture. But this means that he probably thought of his readers as Greek-speaking Jews *who knew something about Hebrew.*

Such people existed throughout the Roman Empire in the first century—Paul would be a prime example—but the largest concentration of them would have occurred in Hellenistic Jewish communities close to Palestine. The region surrounding Antioch of Syria, some three hundred air miles north of Jerusalem, seems especially fitting as a destination for Matthew's Gospel. Antioch was the home of a thriving Christian church that contained both Jews and Gentiles. During Paul's time it tended to align itself with the conservative leadership of James in Jerusalem (Gal. 2:11–13; Acts 15). Emissaries from James produced something of a split between Jewish and Gentile Christians in Antioch by encouraging the former to practice a separate table fellowship (including the Lord's Supper?), presumably to maintain ritual purity (Gal. 2:11–14). This fact gives rise to speculation that some of Antioch's Jewish Christians would have continued to worship in synagogues. As for the non-Christian Jewish population of Antioch, it seems to have cultivated relationships with the rabbinic teachers of Palestine after the war with Rome. This meant, among other things, following their lead on ritual and legal matters.[3] As we shall see, Matthew presupposes that the Jewish Christians to whom he writes find themselves locked in conflict with people who support and embody such rabbinic, i.e., Pharisaic, authority.

When did Matthew write? Most scholars today propose a time after 70 on the grounds that (*a*) Matthew uses Mark's outline, itself written in the late 60s, and that (*b*) Matthew's version of the wedding feast parable (22:1–14) reflects the destruction of Jerusalem. In this story Matthew has Jesus tell of a king who gives a wedding feast for his son. To his consternation the king finds his invitations refused and his messengers killed by those who are supposed to be his honored guests. Unique to Matthew are the following words from the parable: "The king was angry, and he sent his troops and destroyed those murderers and burned their city" (22:7). The thesis that Matthew has allegorized this parable to fit recent events in Jerusalem makes a good deal of sense.

A few other sayings of Jesus found in Matthew also suggest a post-70 date. For example, when the Matthean Jesus looks forward prophetically to Jerusalem's tragic fate, he laments:

> How often would I have gathered your children together as a hen gathers her brood under her wings, and you would not! Behold, your house [probably the Temple] is forsaken and desolate. (Mt. 23:37–38; there is no parallel passage in Mark)

This saying is followed directly by another:

> Jesus left the temple and was going away, when his disciples came to point out to him the buildings of the temple. But he answered them, "You see all these, do you not? Truly, I say to you, there will not be left here one stone upon another, that will not be thrown down." (Mt. 24:1–2)

Mark's version of the same exchange reads:

> And as he came out of the temple, one of his disciples said to him, "Look, Teacher, what wonderful stones and what wonderful buildings!" And Jesus said to him, "Do you see these great buildings? There will not be left here one stone upon another, that will not be thrown down." (Mk. 13:1–2)

In Mark, "these great buildings" could be understood to mean buildings *outside* the Temple precinct in the adjacent city. Matthew, however, makes it clear that the prophecy about leveling referred specifically to "the buildings of the temple." This is a more accurate description of what actually happened, for after Jerusalem's capture by the Romans in 70, a few of the city towers were allowed to stand, while the Temple complex itself was reduced to rubble (Josephus, *The Jewish War*, VI. ix. 1). Finally, Mt. 24:3 looks like a modification of Mk. 13:3f. that would have been made after 70. The two passages go as follows:

> And as [Jesus] sat on the Mount of Olives opposite the temple, Peter and James and John and Andrew asked him privately, "Tell us, when will this be, and what will be the sign when these things are all to be accomplished?" (Mk. 13:3–4)

> As he sat on the Mount of Olives, the disciples came to him privately, saying, "Tell us, when will this be, and what will be the sign of your coming and of the close of the age?" (Mt. 24:3)

Mark's version of this question prepares his readers for information about the Temple's destruction. Matthew, on the other hand, announces *two* distinct future times. First comes the destruction of the Temple (referred to in Mt. 24:2); then follows a later period which will culminate in Christ's coming and the close of the age (see 24:23–33). We recall that Mark had already tried to wean his Gentile readers away from the view that the two times would coincide, inasmuch as that is what many of them expected in the late 60s. Matthew, writing after 70, *knows* that the end of the age did not come with the fall of Jerusalem. His purpose is to assure his readers that Jesus had instructed his disciples to anticipate this serialization of God's final plan. In Matthew's view, it is wrong to object that Jesus' cryptic words about the future, well known by now in Jewish as well as Christian circles, have proved inaccurate. Everything is still going according to the divine timetable.

And this, Matthew believes, will shortly bring the present world order to its consummation. Indeed, *very* shortly! Matthew reproduces two sayings from Mark in which Jesus predicts that everything, including his return from heaven as Son of Man, must happen within the generation of those who have heard his preaching in the early 30s (see Mt. 16:28 and 24:34). This fact helps to define an upper limit for the date of Matthew's composition. That is, by 85, people who had heard Jesus speak in 33 when they were twenty years old, would have attained the age of seventy-two. And this was far above average for Jews living in first-century Palestine.

THE EMERGING POWER OF THE PHARISEES

Yet there is reason to believe that Matthew was not written prior to the late 70s. Many scholars now hold that the decision of the Jamnia academy to identify Jewish Christians worshiping in synagogues and exclude them from full membership in official Judaism occurred about 85.[4] It is hard to tell whether such an edict has actually befallen the congregation(s) to which Matthew writes. On the one hand, he alone preserves a saying of Jesus that pronounces Pharisaic authority legitimate and even counsels submission to it:

"Then said Jesus to the crowds and to his disciples, 'The scribes and the Pharisees sit on Moses' seat; so practice and observe whatever they tell you' " (23:1–3). One might argue that this statement could have no meaning in Christian congregations that had already split off from the synagogue. On the other hand, the same word of Jesus continues as follows:

> . . . but not what they do; for they preach, but do not practice. They bind heavy burdens, hard to bear, and lay them on men's shoulders; but they themselves will not move them with their finger. (Mt. 23:3–4; contrast 11:28, unique to Matthew)

This could be a hint that the edict has indeed struck and is beginning to take effect in the synagogues where Matthew's readers have been worshiping.[5] Such a hypothesis finds support in the fierce, prolonged "woes" against the scribes and Pharisees which form the rest of ch. 23. Though presented to Matthew's readers as words spoken by Jesus to the Pharisees of his day, they have surely been expanded and brought "up to date" so as to reflect post-70 struggles between Jewish Christians and the developing power of the academy at Jamnia.

Consider, for example, this polemic by "Jesus"—found only in Matthew's Gospel:

> [The scribes and Pharisees] love . . . being called rabbi by men. But you are not to be called rabbi, for you have one teacher, and you are all brethren. And call no man your father on earth, for you have one Father, who is in heaven. Neither be called masters, for you have one master, the Christ. (Mt. 23:6–10)

Taken as a whole, Mt. 23:1–10 sounds like advice given to messianic Jews who wish to retain membership in synagogues but find Judaism under the Pharisaic leadership at Jamnia to be more and more unfriendly to their proclamation of Jesus as the Christ.

Supporting this hypothesis are several facts. On numerous occasions Matthew introduces Pharisaic opponents into the Marcan controversy stories he has inherited (9:11; 12:24, 38; 21:45; 22:34, 41). He also transmits—or perhaps constructs—additional material, not found in Mark or Luke, which denounces the righteousness of the

Pharisees or implicates them in plots against Jesus (5:20; 12:14; 21:45f.; 22:15; 23:31; 27:62ff.). In addition, Matthew refers to "their synagogues" (4:23; 9:35; 10:17; 12:9; 13:54; see also 23:34), as if to suggest a Pharisaic takeover, and to "their scribes" (7:29), whom he contrasts with scribes "trained for the kingdom of heaven" (13:52) and sent by Jesus (23:34). These details suggest that whether or not they have actually left their local synagogues, the Christian Jews addressed by Matthew are already building up a teaching office of their own to parallel that of the Jamnia academy.[6] By the time our Evangelist writes, Christian scribes may well be battling against pro-Jamnia leaders in their local communities.[7] Thus, only in Matthew's Gospel do we find Jesus saying:

> Therefore I send you [scribes and Pharisees] prophets and wise men and scribes, some of whom you will kill and crucify, and some you will scourge in your synagogues and persecute from town to town. (Mt. 23:34)

The first readers of these words would probably have taken them as a prophecy coming to fulfillment in their own trying situation.

THE JUDAISM OF MATTHEW'S COMMUNITY

Not for a moment do Matthew and his Christian readers consider themselves apostates from Judaism. The Matthean Jesus has come to fulfill the Law and the Prophets, to uphold the covenant given through Moses and not to abolish it (5:17; 26:28). Only in Matthew does Jesus tell his disciples:

> Truly, I say to you, till heaven and earth pass away, not an iota, not a dot, will pass from the law until all is accomplished. Whoever then relaxes one of the least of these commandments and teaches men so, shall be called least in the kingdom of heaven; but he who does them and teaches them shall be called great in the kingdom of heaven. (Mt. 5:18-19)

Matthew and his community are law-abiding Jews (23:1-3, 23). They want to show their skeptical kinfolk that precisely from a *legal* standpoint, Jesus is "king of the Jews" (2:2). For Matthew, Jesus has not only fulfilled all the messianic prophecies in the Torah; he has also

interpreted and enacted all its laws in their most complete sense (see
3:15; 8:1–4, 16f.; 12:1–3; 15:1–20; 17:24–27; 21:10–17; 22:34–40;
26:17–19). According to Matthew, Jesus frequently crossed verbal
swords with Jewish leaders over questions of oral tradition and personal behavior. But never did he call Scriptural commandments into
question (contrast Mt. 15:1–20 with Mk. 7:1–23). In fact, by means
of the so-called antitheses in the Sermon on the Mount, which are
transmitted only by Matthew, Jesus tightens up the demands of
Torah, making them even stricter than the Pharisees of his day did.
One example will suffice:

> You have heard that it was said to the men of old, "You shall not kill; and
> whoever kills shall be liable to judgment" [Ex. 20:13; Deut. 5:17]. But I
> say to you that every one who is angry with his brother shall be liable to
> judgment; whoever insults his brother shall be liable to the council, and
> whoever says, "You fool!" shall be liable to the hell of fire. (Mt. 5:21–22;
> see also 5:27–30, 31–32, 33–37, 38–42, 43–48)

Matthew assumes that his readers, like Jesus, will be debating with
Jewish opponents well schooled in Torah. Being a Jew of scribal bent
himself (see 13:52 and note 7), he feels strongly that the Messiahship
of Jesus must be demonstrated to Jews by means of argumentation
from the written and the oral law. In his Gospel, therefore, he
provides his readers textbook advice for strengthening their arguments. To serve this purpose, Matthew's "formula quotations" stress
the fulfillment of Scriptural prophecies, while his Jesus sayings function as definitive interpretations of divine commandments (see especially chs. 5–7; 10; 13; 18; 23–24, plus 11:25–30; 15:1–20; 19:1–12;
22:34–40, and Jesus' Great Commission in 28:19f., which closes the
Gospel: "Go therefore and make disciples of all nations, . . . teaching
them to observe all that I have commanded you"). If Matthew's
arrangement of the Sermon on the Mount is meant to be a table of
instructions for the sanctification of life in which Jesus appears as a
rabbi,[8] then we may call the Gospel as a whole Matthew's Mishnah.
It is his book of guidance for Jewish Christians, based on the life and
teachings of Jesus.

It is clear, then, that Matthew makes vigorous efforts to equip

Jewish Christians for effective debate with Jews over the question of Jesus' Messiahship. But this means that for him the Christian mission to Israel must continue. Matthew has by no means given up on persuading Jews that the messianic Judaism of Jesus is the true Judaism. In the light of this concern for mission we may clarify an obscure prophecy of Jesus which appears only in Matthew's Gospel. According to 10:23, Jesus sends out his disciples as missionaries with the words:

> When they persecute you in one town, flee to the next; for truly, I say to you, you will not have gone through all the towns of Israel, before the Son of man comes. (Mt. 10:23)

If Matthew had intended this prophecy of Jesus' final coming to apply *only* to the twelve disciples of his earthly ministry, then he would have transmitted an unfulfillable saying. But the Evangelist is not so naive as to hang himself on such a literal interpretation. He surely understands these words as a message to the Jewish Christians of his day. In Matthew's view, Jesus is speaking to *all* Jewish disciples, not just the original twelve (see 10:16–22). Like those first followers, the missionaries of Matthew's time must also proceed from town to town in Israel, announcing the good news of the Kingdom (10:5–10). Matthew probably interprets Jesus' prophecy to mean: "You will not have *exhausted* [the Greek word is *telesēte*, which literally means "bring to an end"] all the towns of Israel before the Son of Man comes."[9] Thus, the meaning here is not that some of Israel's towns will still have to be evangelized by Christian preachers before Jesus can return as Messiah-King. Instead, Matthew wants to assure his readers that as Christian missionaries continue to visit and revisit these towns, some Jews will always be moved to accept their message and receive them hospitably, right up to the close of the age (10:9–15).

ISRAEL'S LEADERSHIP CONTESTED

Matthew has not given up on convincing the Jewish people of Jesus' Messiahship. To be sure, he nowhere predicts that large numbers of them will become Christians, "for the gate is narrow and the way is hard, that leads to life, and those who find it are few" (Mt. 7:14; contrast Lk. 13:24). Matthew senses the growing power of the academy at Jamnia to win over the people's loyalty. But he hardly shows himself discouraged by this trend, for he believes that the end of the age is near. At Jesus' return, all Jews will see with their own eyes where the true power lies. And this, the Christians already know:

> Jesus said to [the disciples], "Truly, I say to you, in the new world, when the Son of man shall sit on his glorious throne, you who have followed me will also sit on twelve thrones, judging the twelve tribes of Israel." (Mt. 19:28)

No doubt Matthew finds great courage in Jesus' promise and wishes to share this with his readers so that they too may draw strength from it as they face rising opposition from Jewish leaders. Matthew's message is something like this: "Things are not what they seem. Those now being labeled apostates from Judaism (Christians) will soon appear in glory as Israel's true leaders."

This eschatological hope sheds light on Matthew's version of the parable of the vineyard. Mark ended his narration of the parable with these words of Jesus, directed against the chief priests, scribes, and elders:

> Have you not read this scripture:
> "The very stone which the builders rejected
> has become the head of the corner;
> this was the Lord's doing,
> and it is marvelous in our eyes"? (Mk. 12:10–11)

Matthew repeats this Marcan saying almost verbatim, but then he adds the following words, unique to his Gospel:

> "Therefore I tell you, the kingdom of God will be taken away from you and given to a nation producing the fruits of it."
> When the chief priests *and the Pharisees* heard his parables, they perceived that he was speaking about them. (Mt. 21:43, 45, italics added; v. 44 is not contained in many of the best Greek manuscripts)

Matthew wants this parable to tell his readers how the Kingdom (God's rule) will depart from Israel's current leadership (the Jamnia Pharisees) and come to reside with "a nation producing the fruits of it" (the church). This will happen when Jesus returns from heaven as Son of Man (see 19:28, cited above). A careful look at the text shows that Matthew has no intention of declaring either Israel or Judaism obsolete. Nor does he proclaim the church a "new Israel" replacing the Jewish people as God's chosen nation, now or in the age to come. What Matthew does foresee is that in the new world God's reign will be disclosed to Israel (the vineyard) through the agency of Christians, especially Jewish Christians (19:28).

This message causes great offense to modern Jews. They must reject it as condescending. Jews who believe in a messianic era characterized by the reassembling of Israel's twelve ancient tribes hardly expect it to be presided over by Christians. There is no way to blunt this sharp edge; it represents an obvious difference in the future hopes of two great faiths. The last words attributed to Jesus in Matthew's parable of the vineyard (21:43), plus the Evangelist's description of the parable's intended target (21:45), have probably developed out of conflicts between Jewish Christians and the Pharisaic leadership at Jamnia in the 70s and 80s of the first century. We Christians must honestly ponder whether such judgments are appropriate to the Christian gospel in our day.

THE WAY TO SALVATION

An equally difficult passage from the standpoint of contemporary Jewish-Christian dialogue occurs in Mt. 11:25–27. Having warned the Galilean cities of Chorazin, Bethsaida, and Capernaum to expect harsh treatment on the day of judgment for ignoring the import of his miraculous deeds (11:20–24), Jesus then turns abruptly to prayer and speaks these words aloud:

I thank thee, Father, Lord of heaven and earth, that thou hast hidden these things from the wise and understanding and revealed them to babes; yea, Father, for such was thy gracious will. All things have been delivered

to me by my Father; and no one knows the Son except the Father, and
no one knows the Father except the Son and any one to whom the Son
chooses to reveal him. (Mt. 11:25–27)

For Matthew, "these things" probably refers to the meaning of Jesus'
mighty works (see 11:20). Not the "wise and understanding" (Israel's
official leaders), but only "babes" (the common, uneducated folk)
have been permitted to discern in Jesus' ministry signs of the dawning
Kingdom. Here we encounter the same "blindness" motif which we
found earlier in Paul and Mark (Rom. 11:7–10; Mk. 4:10–12). According to this notion, God is responsible for Israel's widespread
refusal to accept Jesus' mission. In 11:27, however, Matthew moves
beyond Paul and Mark by presenting Jesus as the solitary guardian
of God's will, and even of God's identity. The clear implication is
that no individual Jews can know God as Father unless Jesus allows
it. This claim would constitute something like blasphemy among
ordinary Jews in the time of Jesus and Matthew. Insofar as it is taken
literally by modern Christians, it obviously serves to widen the gap
between them and God's ancient people.

Matthew appears to soften his hard line just a bit by following v.
27 with this now-famous invitation of Jesus:

Come to me, all who labor and are heavy laden, and I will give you rest.
Take my yoke upon you, and learn from me; for I am gentle and lowly
in heart, and you will find rest for your souls. For my yoke is easy, and my
burden is light. (Mt. 11:28–30)

These words of Jesus are unique to Matthew's Gospel. At first reading, the invitation sounds quite magnanimous and open-ended. But
what about those who do not feel heavy-laden or burdened with the
Torah yoke? What about those who feel that they already know God
as Father through the wisdom of Judaism?[10] We Christians must not
allow these difficult questions to slip through our consciousness too
easily.

Perhaps the most we can say is that Matthew himself demonstrates
some flexibility in describing *how* one comes to Jesus and gets to
know the Father through him. This coming and knowing is clearly
not reducible to one's public confession of Jesus as Messiah. In

7:21–23 Matthew's Jesus denounces so-called Christians who call him Lord and even do mighty works in his name. For unspecified reasons, however, they remain "evildoers" in his sight who will not enter the Kingdom of Heaven. Again, Matthew alone tells a story of the Last Judgment in which Jesus the messianic King divides all of earth's people into sheep (the righteous) and goats (the evildoers) on the basis of whether they have performed deeds of mercy toward his "brothers" (25:31–46). As the King puts it, "Truly, I say to you, as you did it to one of the least of these my brethren, you did it to me" (25:40). For Matthew, the decisive way of coming to Jesus is by providing food, drink, and clothing to the needy; comforting visits to the sick and imprisoned; and a warm welcome to strangers (25:34–36; see also 10:40–42). During their lifetime, neither the sheep nor the goats know that the suffering folk they encounter are actually Jesus incognito (25:37, 44).

On the basis of this story we may conclude that for Matthew some of the goats will turn out to be pseudo Christians, while some of the sheep may be Jews who never confessed Jesus as Christ. In Matthew's view, it is not finally one's conscious, outward acceptance of Jesus' Messiahship which saves.[11] Rather, it is a person's repentance from vain perceptions and works to renewed faith in God's power, along with the righteous behavior that flows from this (see, e.g., 4:17; 5:6, 20, 43–48; 6:33; 7:15–27; 9:10–13; 10:40–42; 11:20–21; 12:38–41; 13:36–49; 18:1–4; 19:13–15; 21:18–22, 28–32; 23:23; 24:14–51; 25: 14–30, 31–46). Only those who have specifically denied Jesus "before men" are warned to expect a reciprocal denial of themselves by him before the heavenly throne (10:33; contrast Mk. 8:38, which is not repeated in Matthew). And even this warning must be qualified, for Peter's case proves that a repentance inspired by mercy can save even the public traitor from final condemnation. Like Paul, Matthew leaves the door to eternal life ajar for Jews who cannot believe in Jesus' Messiahship. This may seem to be a small thing, but when we consider the opposition Matthew and his readers were facing from many of their Jewish neighbors, it becomes a magnanimous gesture. The most "natural" thing is to consign all of one's enemies to eternal damnation.

MATTHEW'S BLINDNESS

In this light we may now examine what is probably the harshest judgment upon Israel found anywhere in Matthew's Gospel. Both Matthew and Luke tell of a Gentile centurion who comes to Jesus asking that his sick servant be healed. Humbly declaring his unworthiness to entertain a Jewish prophet in his house, he professes faith in Jesus' power to heal from afar by means of a word (Mt. 8:5–13; Lk. 7:1–10). According to Matthew, Jesus responds to the centurion's speech by telling his disciples:

> Truly, I say to you, not even in Israel have I found such faith. I tell you, many will come from east and west and sit at table with Abraham, Isaac, and Jacob in the kingdom of heaven, while the sons of the kingdom will be thrown into the outer darkness; there men will weep and gnash their teeth. (Mt. 8:10–12)

The clause "while the sons of the kingdom will be thrown into outer darkness" is probably a Matthean addition to an original saying by Jesus.[12] It appears to be nothing other than a wholesale exclusion of unbelieving Jews from the messianic banquet at the end of the age.

Here Matthew apparently reverses his usual procedure. Ordinarily, he distinguishes rather clearly between leaders and people, between Jamnia Judaism and the ancient faith of Israel, with the first members of these two pairs receiving his censure. But in 8:12 Matthew has Jesus casting "the sons of the kingdom" into outer darkness. This phrase probably cannot be restricted to leaders taking the Jamnia line. Its usual meaning in Hebrew would be something like "those destined for the Kingdom" or "those who stand to inherit the Kingdom." Matthew himself uses the phrase this way in 13:38 when referring to Christians. In 8:12 the Evangelist probably wishes to rebuke those Jews who claim the Kingdom as a birthright by virtue of their ancestors (see 3:7–10). But it is by no means certain that these people consist solely of leaders. It seems that Matthew has here allowed his feelings about his opponents to spill over onto the Jewish people as a whole. Let us Christians admit this to our Jewish friends in all honesty. Let us frankly concede that on occasion the canonical

Gospel most often read aloud in our churches distorts the truth about Jesus' attitudes toward Judaism, and vice versa.

A similar distortion shows up in Matthew's version of the passion story. Here Jewish guilt for the death of Jesus is definitely enlarged, while Pilate's is diminished (see the additions to the Marcan outline in Mt. 26:3–4; 27:3–10, 19, 24, 62–66; 28:11–15). Only Matthew, of all the Gospel writers, places into the mouth of the Jewish crowd gathered before Pilate's tribunal those fateful words: "His blood be on us and on our children!" (27:25). To be sure, Matthew connects this self-judgment only with that particular crowd of Jews incited by the high priests to demand Jesus' crucifixion (see 27:20). But the cruel fact is that thousands of Christians down through the centuries have justified their crimes against innocent Jews on the basis of this one unfortunate sentence. Had the church in past centuries been capable of interpreting these Matthean words by means of historical criticism, it might have prevented some of the grotesque offenses committed by its members.

CONCLUSIONS

What shall we say, then, of Matthew? Is he fundamentally anti-Judaistic, or even anti-Semitic? Neither of these labels makes much sense in his case, for Matthew is a Jew writing to Jews. Together, author and readers consider themselves well within the bounds of Judaism, even though the official religious leaders of their day tend more and more to view them as apostate. The situation is not unlike that faced by members of the Qumran community in their confrontations with the priestly Judaism of Jerusalem.

In opposition to his Jamnia opponents, Matthew proposes to show how the acceptance of Jesus' Messiahship by Jews reaffirms, renews, and fulfills the best of Judaism, without destroying any of its essentials. The Evangelist argues that through Jesus the Torah is upheld (5:17–19) and the name of Israel's God magnified (15:29–31). For Matthew, Jesus reigns primarily as King of *Israel* (2:6; 27:42). With great care the Matthean Jesus directs his ministry specifically to Jews (10:5f., 23; 15:24). Messiah and Evangelist alike mourn the destruction of Jerusalem, as all true Jews must (23:37f.; 24:15–22). No matter how great its "blindness" to God's purposes, it remains "the city of the great King" (5:35), "the holy city" (27:53). In sum, we may conclude that Matthew sincerely attempts to honor the people, the traditions, and the institutions of Israel.

Yet we have also seen the other side of this Evangelist's messianic Judaism. Matthew intensifies his polemic against Pharisees far beyond anything occurring in the ministry of the historical Jesus. He lashes out ferociously against that group in Judaism whose rise to power after 70 is causing him and his readers so many problems (see especially ch. 23). On occasion, and contrary to his usual practice (e.g., 9:3, 8), Matthew lumps leaders and people together, warning both groups that severe judgment awaits them in the age to come if they continue to be unmoved by Jesus' ministry (8:11f.; 11:20–24; 23:37–39). These passages probably reflect the hurt and anger suffered in post-70 battles between church and synagogue. In Matthew's Gospel it becomes apparent that the period of mutual toleration between Jews and Jewish Christians is drawing to a close. Each party is hardening its attitudes against the other. The painful break, long a possibility, now becomes almost inevitable.

Perhaps it is impossible from our vantage point in the twentieth century to determine whether Matthew's Gospel represents primarily a contribution to or a development from this historical trend. In either case, we Christians owe it to our Jewish neighbors and ourselves to note that Matthew finds the idea of a non-Jewish Christianity utterly incomprehensible. Though he mandates Jewish believers to missionize Gentiles, the risen Christ of his Great Commission makes it quite clear that converts from the nations must "observe all that I have commanded you" (28:20). And this means Torah *plus*. [13] Matthew was convinced that very soon Jesus would return from heaven to confront all people, Jews and Gentiles alike, with the fullness of *Israel's* heritage. On that day the inhabitants of Jerusalem, presently blinded to his messianic identity, would welcome him with joy, saying: "Blessed is he who comes in the name of the Lord" (23:39).

CHAPTER 5

Luke-Acts: Roots in Israel's History

New Testament scholars have long assumed that a single author produced both our third canonical Gospel and the Acts of the Apostles. Not only is the literary style consistent from the first to the second book, but in both works we find the addressee named Theophilus, a Greek word meaning "lover of God" (Lk. 1:1–4; Acts 1:1). The writer of Acts even refers to a "first book" in which he "dealt with all that Jesus began to do and teach, until the day when he was taken up" (Acts 1:1). This book almost certainly is our Third Gospel.

THE HISTORICAL SITUATION BEHIND LUKE-ACTS

But who is the reader called Theophilus? Is he a Roman official who might be persuaded to favor the Christian movement? Is he a Jew or proselyte to Judaism who desires more accurate information about Jesus and the church than he has yet received? Could he be a literary patron who has promised to publish Luke's two-volume work widely in the ancient world? Or is Theophilus a figurative name for Christians who, in Luke's view, need to "acquire exact knowledge about the reliability of the things concerning which [they] have been instructed" (Lk. 1:4, author's translation)? This last option, which seems to me most likely,[1] does not necessarily exclude the "patron" theory. Theophilus could be a real person and a symbol at the same time. If so, Luke was attempting to communicate both with an individual and, through that person, with a larger group. Because of Luke's clear emphasis on the church's universal mission "to the end of the earth" (Acts 1:8; see also Lk. 14:22–23; 24:45–48; Acts 28:28), some scholars have thought that he considered his larger circle of readers to be primarily Gentiles. But we shall do well to postpone taking a definite stand on this issue until we have become more familiar with the overall content of Luke's two-volume work.

What we can do now is work out a probable thesis about *when* Luke wrote. On two occasions in the Third Gospel, Luke portrays Jesus prophesying the destruction of Jerusalem in words more specific to the actual historical event than anything else found in the New Testament. The texts go as follows:

> And when [Jesus] drew near and saw the city he wept over it, saying, "Would that even today you knew the things that make for peace! But now they are hid from your eyes. For the days shall come upon you, when your enemies will cast up a bank about you and surround you, and hem you in on every side, and dash you to the ground, you and your children within you, and they will not leave one stone upon another in you; because you did not know the time of your visitation." (Lk. 19:41–44)

> But when you see Jerusalem surrounded by armies, then know that its desolation has come near. Then let those who are in Judea flee to the mountains, and let those who are inside the city depart, and let not those who are out in the country enter it; for these are days of vengeance, to fulfil all that is written. Alas for those who are with child and for those who give suck in those days! For great distress shall be upon the earth and wrath upon this people; they will fall by the edge of the sword, and be led captive among all nations; and Jerusalem will be trodden down by the Gentiles, until the times of the Gentiles are fulfilled. (Lk. 21:20–24)

The first passage, which accurately reflects the Roman method of siege used in 70, is unique to Luke's Gospel. The second is Luke's modification of verses from Mark 13. Only Luke's Jesus predicts that Jerusalem will be surrounded by armies. Only he recommends flight to Jews in general rather than to Jewish *Christians,* most of whom would have departed to Pella before the siege began. (Contrast Mt.

24:15ff.; Mk. 13:14ff. and compare Lk. 23:27-31.) Unique to Luke's Gospel is Jesus' prophecy that "this people" (the Jews) will suffer captivity or death by sword and that "Jerusalem will be trodden down by the Gentiles, until the times of the Gentiles are fulfilled" (21:24). We shall return to this verse below. Here we want to highlight that it clearly presupposes an extended period of Gentile rule over Jerusalem *after* the city's destruction (see also 21:6). Matthew and Mark do not envision this.

All things considered, Luke's editing of the prophecies by Jesus concerning Jerusalem's destruction argues for a post-70 knowledge of the event. In other words, both the Third Gospel and its sequel, Acts, came into being sometime after the Jewish war with Rome. But how long afterward? There are some data to help us answer this question. For one thing, Luke purposely dilutes the passages in Mark which his readers might take as predictions of an *imminent* Parousia (contrast Mt. 16:28; Mk. 9:1 with Lk. 9:27 and Mt. 24:34-36; Mk. 13:30-32 with Lk. 21:32-33). Moreover, Luke adds sayings of Jesus (not found elsewhere) which downplay an apocalyptic coming of the Kingdom in the near future (Lk. 17:20-21; 19:11ff.; Acts 1:6-7). This gives some basis for concluding that Luke wrote several years after the Jewish-Roman war when some believers had begun to get impatient about the "delay" of Jesus' triumphal return from heaven. Luke addresses this uneasiness with a word spoken to the Twelve by the risen Christ just prior to his ascension:

> It is not for you to know times or seasons which the Father has fixed by his own authority. But you shall receive power when the Holy Spirit has come upon you; and you shall be my witnesses in Jerusalem and in all Judea and Samaria and to the end of the earth. (Acts 1:7-8)

SALVATION HISTORY IN STAGES

Let us turn now to Luke's overall organization of his two-volume work, giving special attention to what this may reveal about his attitudes toward Jews and Judaism. One of Luke's most obvious intentions is to divide world history into a series of stages in God's plan

of salvation, beginning with the birth of John the Baptist and leading up to Paul's arrival in Rome about the year 62. On this we find
among contemporary scholars a virtual consensus. Scholars disagree,
however, on the exact number of these stages. For our purposes, it
will be best to examine the three most prominent stages and modify
them when evidence from Luke or Acts warrants such adjustments.[2]

Stage One may be characterized as the era of the Law and the
Prophets. This includes Israel's entire history from Abraham's call to
the ministry of John the Baptist (Lk. 16:16). Luke sees much that is
good in this period. For example, he applauds God's choice of Israel
as his special people (Acts 7:1ff.; 13:16ff.). Unlike Paul, Luke speaks
highly of Moses and the giving of the Law (Lk. 16:17; Acts 7:20–44,
53). According to the third Evangelist, God has acted mercifully
throughout Israel's history to "remember his holy covenant" by saving his people from their enemies (Lk. 1:68–74). In his birth narratives (Lk. 1–2), Luke identifies as "righteous before God" the law-
abiding Jews Zechariah, Elizabeth, Mary, Joseph, Simeon, and Anna.
On the negative side, Luke notes that Stage One has witnessed
frequent rebellions by God's people against the law and the prophets
(Lk. 11:47–48; 13:34; Acts 7:27–29, 35–43, 51–53).

Stage Two commences with the preaching of John the Baptist (Lk.
1:80; 3:1ff.; 16:16). In narrating John's ministry, Luke wishes to show
that God has now brought his word to Israel in a new way. Jesus, of
course, soon takes over the torch from John and becomes the domi-
nant figure. Thus we can justifiably call Stage Two "the time of
Jesus." It is important to notice that Stage Two does not cancel out
Stage One. Rather, Two enfolds One and raises it to new heights.
God has not forsaken Israel as his chosen people. The Law and the
Prophets remain in force, just as they always did (Lk. 16:17; 24:27,
44). In fact, Jesus even assumes the role of that singular prophet-
like-Moses whom the ancient lawgiver himself had predicted in
Deut. 18:15 (Lk. 13:33; 24:19–21; see also Acts 3:22ff.; 7:37). Luke
argues for a strict continuity in God's developing plan. No promise
made to the chosen people falls by the wayside. In no sense does God
break his ancient covenant with Israel. Yet there is also novelty, for
during Stage Two, God concentrates all his efforts for the salvation

of Israel into one man, Jesus of Nazareth.

With the ascension of Jesus and the descent of the Holy Spirit at Pentecost a third stage in salvation history begins. We may call Stage Three "the time of the church." During this period Jesus resides in heaven, anticipating his return to earth as reigning Messiah (Acts 3:20–21; 7:55–56; 9:3ff.). But he does not wait passively; nor is he far away. Through the power of his name and the Spirit which he has poured out upon all his followers he intervenes miraculously in the lives of individuals and leads his church forward in mission (Acts 3:1–16; 4:29ff.; 5:19ff.; 9:1–18; 10:44ff.; 13:1ff.; 16:6–10; 18:9ff.; 22:17–21).

Stage Three continues throughout the book of Acts, and even beyond, for with the conclusion of his second book Luke brings church history into the lifetime of his audience. The last scene in Acts depicts Paul's preaching the gospel to the Jewish leaders in Rome. Then, following their mixed reception, he prophesies (in the words of Is. 6:9–10) that the Christian movement will continue as a predominantly Gentile phenomenon (Acts 28:17–30). Luke's final words refer to Paul's two-year residence in the capital city during which he "welcomed all who came to him, preaching the kingdom of God and teaching about the Lord Jesus Christ quite openly and unhindered" (Acts 28:17–31). With the conclusion of Acts, Luke's readers must take up *their* roles in Stage Three. Christ's mission continues, and now they themselves are the missionaries.

Like the transition from Stage One to Stage Two, so also the change from Two to Three involves not the negation of the past but its embrace by the present. Thus Luke pictures the earliest church in Jerusalem as a community composed exclusively of Torah-honoring Jews who frequent the Temple for worship. Similarly, the Paul of Acts identifies himself throughout his ministry as an orthodox Jew, a practicing Pharisee faithful not only to the commandments of Torah but even to the traditions of the fathers (Acts 21:17–26; 22:3; 23:6; 24:12–17; 26:4–31; 28:17–19). While Luke notes that the followers of Jesus have come to be called by the name "Christian" (Acts 11:26; 26:28), he himself prefers other descriptions (e.g. "disciples" or "believers"). For him, the church represents not a new religion—

the word "Christianity" occurs nowhere in the New Testament—but a righteous remnant within Judaism (Acts 28:17–22). This is the meaning of Luke's distinctive term for Christ's church: "the Way" (Acts 9:2; 16:17; 18:25f.; 19:9, 23; 22:4; 24:14, 22). In his view, the story of the church represents the climactic phase of *Israel's* history. Even as he tells stories about Gentiles who are beginning to join "the Way" in large numbers, Luke makes clear that Jews and Jewish Christians enjoy a certain precedence. Thus, nearly every missionary venture undertaken by Luke's Paul begins with the proclamation of the gospel to Jews, usually in synagogues. This holds true even after particular Jews at a given location have rejected the message. For example, when Paul and Barnabas meet stiff opposition to their preaching from certain Jews in Antioch of Pisidia (although many Jews believed; see 13:43), they respond with what appears to be a programmatic rejection of their opponents:

> It was necessary that the word of God be spoken first to you. Since you thrust it from you, and judge yourselves unworthy of eternal life, behold, we turn to the Gentiles. (Acts 13:46)

These words sound quite final and cosmic. But in fact this turning to the Gentiles is understood by Luke as nothing more than a temporary shift in Paul's missionary strategy. Just seven verses later we read: "Now at Iconium they entered together into the Jewish synagogue, and so spoke that a great company believed, both of Jews and of Greeks" (14:1). This pattern prevails through Acts. For Luke, it is incorrect to speak about *Israel's* rejection of the gospel. Instead, he sees the empirical Israel of Paul's day as God's "divided people."[3] Some Jews disbelieve; others at different times and places accept Jesus' Messiahship. Toward the end of Acts, James refers to "many thousands" of Jewish believers who "are all zealous for the law" (21:20).

CHURCH HISTORY AS ISRAEL'S HISTORY

These *Jewish Christians* represent the chief actors in the drama narrated by the author of Acts. Peter, John, Stephen, Barnabas, Silas, Timothy, Philip, Mark, James the brother of Jesus, Priscilla, Aquila,

Apollos, and above all Paul—each one is pictured as a Jew absolutely faithful to the laws and traditions of Israel. For Luke, belief in Jesus does not make Jews into apostates from their mother faith. Indeed, when we examine the references in Acts to *Gentile* Christians, we discover that most of them who command Luke's attention were proselytes to Judaism or worshipers of Israel's God prior to their conversions. Here we may call to mind Nicolaus of Antioch (Acts 6:5), the Ethiopian eunuch (8:26–40), the Roman centurion Cornelius (ch. 10), Lydia, the seller of purple (16:11–15), and Titius Justus (18:5–7).[4]

How can we explain Luke's efforts to accent the Jewishness of the early church? We might conclude that Luke is simply telling history the way it was. There is much truth in this thesis. But if we take it as the whole truth, we run into problems. The orthodox, Pharisaic Paul whom Luke presents in Acts is not easily reconciled with the freewheeling ex-Pharisee of the Pauline letters. We recall that this Paul wrote:

> If any other man thinks he has reason for confidence in the flesh, I have more: circumcised on the eighth day, of the people of Israel, of the tribe of Benjamin, a Hebrew born of Hebrews; as to the law a Pharisee, as to zeal a persecutor of the church, as to righteousness under the law blameless. But whatever gain I had, I counted as loss for the sake of Christ. Indeed I count everything as loss because of the surpassing worth of knowing Christ Jesus my Lord. For his sake I have suffered the loss of all things, and count them as refuse, in order that I may gain Christ and be found in him, not having a righteousness of my own, based on law, but that which is through faith in Christ, the righteousness from God that depends on faith. (Phil. 3:4–9)

> For though I am free from all men, I have made myself a slave to all, that I might win the more. To the Jews I became as a Jew, in order to win Jews; to those under the law I became as one under the law—though not being myself under the law—that I might win those under the law. To those outside the law I became as one outside the law—not being without law toward God but under the law of Christ—that I might win those outside the law. (1 Cor. 9:19–21)

> For being ignorant of the righteousness that comes from God, and seeking
> to establish their own, they [the Jews] did not submit to God's righteous-
> ness. For Christ is the end of the law for righteousness to everyone who
> believes. (Rom. 10:3–4; author's translation)

It is possible that Luke knew Paul only later in his career when his
attitudes toward Judaism had mellowed even more than we see in
Romans 9–11. But then we would have to say that Luke reconstructed
the entire ministry of Paul according to the image of the elder apostle;
and this can be no more than speculation. Thus, inasmuch as Luke
organizes his two-volume work by distinguishing successive epochs in
Israel's history, we should probably concede that he sometimes edits
early Christian history in order to stress its continuities with Judaism.
Such a view would account not only for the super-Jewish Paul of Acts
but also for Luke's conscious imitation of the style of the Greek Old
Testament or LXX throughout his two-volume work.[5]

But *why* did Luke wish to tell Christian history in such a Jewish
way? A recent work by the Swedish scholar Jacob Jervell helps us at
this point. Jervell sees that the speech by James the brother of Jesus
before the Apostolic Council reveals Luke's own thinking about the
relationship between Israel and the Christian movement. In this
speech James justifies preaching the gospel to the Gentiles as follows:

> Simeon [Peter] has related how God first visited the Gentiles, to take out
> of them a people for his name [the reference is to Peter's story about the
> conversion of Cornelius in Acts 10–11]. And with this the words of the
> prophets agree, as it is written,
>   "After this I will return,
>   and I will rebuild the dwelling of David,
>   which has fallen;
>   I will rebuild its ruins,
>   and I will set it up,
>   that the rest of men may seek the Lord,
>   and all the Gentiles who are called
>   by my name,
>   says the Lord, who has made these things
>   known from of old." (Acts 15:14–18)

According to Jervell, the James of Acts here points to a common expectation in first-century Judaism: namely, that when the Messiah begins to restore Israel, many Gentiles will join the holy people to participate in their good fortune and worship the true God.[6] On this hypothesis, "the dwelling of David" (15:16) means the Jews of the first century, the empirical people of Israel. It would follow that Luke sees Israel being "rebuilt" by God through Jesus the son of David, particularly through the Holy Spirit which Jesus pours out on his followers at Pentecost. Jesus himself received this "promise of the Holy Spirit" on the Davidic throne in heaven at the time of his ascension (Acts 2:22–36). Jervell's view is further illustrated in that both the Ethiopian eunuch and Cornelius, the first two Gentile converts in Acts, are portrayed as "seeking" the Lord Jesus (15:17) through Philip and Peter respectively (8:26–38; 10:4–8, 17–23). These two Jewish Christians presumably stand for Israel in process of restoration. According to Luke, the twelve apostles in Jerusalem are already beginning to enact their role as judges over the tribes of Israel, thus fulfilling Jesus' prophecy at the Last Supper (Lk. 22:30). Unlike Matthew, who sees the judgeship of the Twelve inaugurated only at the Final Judgement (compare Mt. 19:28 with Mt. 25:31ff.), Luke has Jesus locate this "in my kingdom" (Lk. 22:30).[7] This Kingdom, which is Jesus' messianic reign, has already commenced with his ascension to the Davidic throne in heaven (Acts 2:29–36; 17:7).

Additional evidence that Luke equates Jewish Christians with restored Israel is to be found in Acts 15:19–21. Here James renders judgment about which Jewish laws Gentile believers must obey in order to live in community with Jewish believers:

> We should not trouble those of the Gentiles who turn to God, but should write to them to abstain from the pollutions of idols and from unchastity and from what is strangled and from blood. For from early generations Moses has had in every city those who preach him, for he is read every sabbath in the synagogues. (Acts 15:19–21)

Two things may be said about this decision. First, it presupposes a church situation in which believers must be sensitive to the rules for fellowship between Jews and Gentiles as they are practiced *in the synagogues.* This suggests ongoing Christian contact with synagogues at the time Luke wrote. Second, the actual rules cited by James represent commands from the Old Testament which were imposed upon Gentile peoples residing within the borders of ancient Israel (see Lev. 17:10ff.; 18:26).[8] These were variously named "sojourners" or "strangers."

In the light of this evidence, it seems best to agree with Jervell that Luke conceives of Gentile believers not as part of Israel itself but as an "associate" people of God.[9] Jewish Christians are Israel-being-restored and as such, the foundation of the church. To them, Gentiles come for a share in salvation (Acts 26:17–18). But this salvation is derivatory. It issues forth from *the* people of God (Jews) to create *a* people of God (Gentile believers; see Acts 15:14). It is not that Luke wishes to relegate Gentiles to second-class citizenship in the church, but, in line with his overall program, he strives to demonstrate God's faithfulness first of all to *Israel.*

Never in Luke-Acts does the church supersede Israel or become its substitute. Never is the church (even the Jewish church) called "new Israel" or "true Israel." Instead, every occurrence of the word "Israel" in Luke's two-volume work denotes the Jewish nation as a whole, without regard to whether it believes or rejects the gospel. For Luke, Israel always means something historically and ethnically Jewish. Yet he also sees something transcendent in the reality called Israel, for he uses the word most often in contexts that envision God's efforts to lead his chosen people forward (Lk. 1:16, 54, 68, 80; 2:25, 32, 34; 22:30; 24:21; Acts 1:6; 2:36; 4:10; 5:21; 7:23, 37; 9:15; 10:36; 13:16–41). For Luke, there is a certain futurity or potentiality built into the term. Israel, the chosen and beloved people of God, can become even more than it presently is.

This future thrust shows up at the end of Acts when Paul enters Rome as a refugee from the Jewish leaders in Jerusalem and a prisoner of the Romans. Neither of these conditions, however, diverts him from his mission to Israel (see 9:15). Three days after his arrival in the capital city he calls together the local Jewish leaders and tells them:

Brethren, though I had done nothing against the people or the customs of our fathers, yet I was delivered prisoner from Jerusalem into the hands of the Romans. When they had examined me, they wished to set me at liberty, because there was no reason for the death penalty in my case. But when the Jews objected, I was compelled to appeal to Caesar—though I had no charge to bring against my nation. For this reason therefore I have asked to see you and speak with you, since it is because of the *hope of Israel* that I am bound with this chain. (Acts 28:17–20, italics added)

Earlier, in a speech to King Agrippa, this "hope of Israel" looks toward "the promise made by God to our fathers, to which our twelve tribes hope to attain, as they earnestly worship night and day" (Acts 26:6–7). In Acts, Israel's hope is probably to be thought of as its final appropriation of the holy land at the general resurrection, with all the blessings that attend this. Like the Paul of Romans 9–11, Luke's apostle to the Gentiles sees a direct, positive relationship between his ministry and the future longings of his kinspeople by race.

STAGE FOUR IN GOD'S SALVATION

In some ways Luke makes the final establishment of God's Kingdom more explicitly Jewish than Paul does in his letters. Recently, Arthur Wainwright has shown that Luke envisions a quite materialistic restoration of the Kingdom to Israel. Thus, Luke's Jesus predicts that "Jerusalem will be trodden down by the Gentiles, until the times of the Gentiles are fulfilled" (Lk. 21:24; a passage unique to the Third Gospel). This prophecy suggests that at some future time Jerusalem will rise from its ashes and stand once again under Jewish rule.[10] This appears to presuppose a fourth stage in salvation history to follow after the time of the church. Further evidence for such a fourth stage appears in Luke's expectation that Jesus' return from heaven as glorious Son of Man will mean not the instantaneous end of history but the beginning of a new period of time on earth when "redemption is drawing near" (21:27–28). In other words, Luke thinks that the Parousia will inaugurate, but not conclude, the final coming of God's Kingdom.

Consistent with this interpretation is Luke's account of a conversation between the risen Christ and his disciples immediately prior to the ascension:

> So when they had come together, they asked him, "Lord, will you at this time restore the kingdom to Israel?" He said to them, "It is not for you to know times or seasons which the Father has fixed by his own authority. But you shall receive power when the Holy Spirit has come upon you; and you shall be my witnesses in Jerusalem and in all Judea and Samaria and to the end of the earth." (Acts 1:6–8)

It is important to notice that Jesus rebukes not the question about the restoration of the Kingdom as such but rather the impatience that prompts it. Luke assumes that Israel will inherit God's Kingdom in an earthly sense (see Acts 1:11). However, the Kingdom cannot begin to come in this final manner until the church's missionary preaching has spread to the very "end of the earth"—in other words, until Stage Three of salvation history has drawn to a close.

Luke expresses much the same idea later in Acts when he shows Peter urging the Jews in Jerusalem to repent so that

> times of refreshing may come from the presence of the Lord, and that he may send the Christ appointed for you, Jesus, whom heaven must receive until the time for establishing [literally: "restoring"] all that God spoke by the mouth of his holy prophets from of old. (Acts 3:19–21)

And what *did* God speak through his ancient prophets concerning Israel's restoration? Wainwright calls attention to several prophetic promises which were probably common knowledge among first-century Jews:

   a) the rescue of the holy land from foreign domination (Jer. 16:15; 24:6; 50:19).
   b) the fruitful blossoming of the land (Isa. 65:9ff.).
   c) the return of the ten lost tribes of Jacob (Sir. 48:10).
   d) the reconciliation of fathers to children, and vice versa (Mal. 4:6).
   e) the rehabilitation of Jerusalem, particularly the temple (Dan. 8:9–14).[11]

Clearly, Luke wants to point his Christian readers toward these earthly expectations of first-century Jews. In doing so, he looks forward to a fourth stage of salvation history when Israel will find its classical hopes realized in God's Kingdom.

NON-CHRISTIAN JEWS IN STAGE FOUR

An important question arises at this point. Does Luke think that Jews who have rejected Jesus' Messiahship will be permitted to enter this restored Israel-in-the-Kingdom? Luke is hardly a universalist by modern standards. He does not believe, for example, that all Gentiles will be saved. Only those "ordained to eternal life" (Acts 13:48) can believe and enter the church. With Jews, however, the issue becomes more complicated. On the one hand, Luke applies the name "Israel" even to unbelieving Jews (Lk. 7:9; Acts 4:10, 27; 5:21, 31; 7:42). As Jervell correctly notes, Israel in the time of the church becomes a people divided. On the other hand, Luke's Peter dangles a dire threat over the Jews of Jerusalem in one of his missionary speeches:

> Repent therefore, and turn again, that your sins may be blotted out, that times of refreshing may come from the presence of the Lord. . . . Moses said, "The Lord God will raise up for you a prophet [Jesus] from your brethren as he raised me up. You shall listen to him in whatever he tells you. And it shall be that every soul that does not listen to that prophet shall be destroyed [literally *exolethreuthēsetai* means "rooted out"] from the people." (Acts 3:19, 22–23)

This passage can only mean that by not hearing and obeying Jesus the Mosaic prophet-Messiah Jews will forfeit their place in a renewed Israel.

Luke makes a similar point in his Gospel with the following story:

> And some one said to [Jesus], "Lord, will those who are saved be few?" And he said to them, "Strive to enter by the narrow door; for many, I tell you, will seek to enter and will not be able. When once the householder has risen up and shut the door, you will begin to stand outside and to knock at the door, saying, 'Lord, open to us.' He will answer you, 'I do not know where you come from.' Then you will begin to say, 'We ate and drank in your presence, and you taught in our streets.' But he will say, 'I tell you, I do not know where you come from; depart from me, all you workers of

iniquity!' There you will weep and gnash your teeth, when you see Abraham and Isaac and Jacob and all the prophets in the kingdom of God and you yourselves thrust out. And men will come from east and west, and north and south, and sit at table in the kingdom of God. And behold, some are last who will be first, and some are first who will be last." (Lk. 13:23–30)

Here those Jews who do not enter God's salvation through the narrow door of repentance are told that they have excluded themselves from the great messianic feast in the Kingdom of God (Stage Four). Yet Luke's version of this saying is somewhat less harsh than Matthew's. The Jesus of this Gospel states quite bluntly that "the sons of the kingdom [unbelieving Jews who expect to inherit the Kingdom?] will be thrown into the outer darkness" (Mt. 8:12). The possibility of repentance is not even mentioned. Luke avoids the universality of this judgment by closing his version of the banquet story with an independent saying of Jesus: "Some are last who will be first, and some are first who will be last" (see Mk. 10:31; Mt. 20:16 for the placement of the saying in other contexts). When seen as a caption on the whole of Lk. 13:23–29, this Lucan addition raises the hope that Jews who are "thrust out" of the Kingdom banquet for not repenting in Stages Two and Three will receive another chance in Stage Four, once the initial shock of exclusion wears off. Perhaps those who stand outside the feast looking in will "come to themselves" and acknowledge their need for reconciliation with the Father, just as the prodigal son did (Lk. 15:17ff.). Perhaps they will yet listen to Jesus when they meet him face-to-face as the glorious Son of Man (12:10). If so, they will reclaim their place in Israel renewed.

Luke's parable of the great banquet allows this possibility, though it appears at first to do exactly the opposite. The parable ends with harsh words of Jesus: "I tell you, none of those men who were invited [presumably Jews who reject his message] shall taste my banquet" (Lk. 14:24). Jesus makes this statement at the home of a Pharisee where he is dining with a group of pious Jews (14:1ff.). The "you" of 14:24 is plural in Greek and suggests that Jesus is speaking directly to his table companions. This would mean that the banquet he refers to is probably his own ministry and (for Luke) its continuation in the life of the

church, not that final feast "in the kingdom of God" (13:28–29).[12]
Luke leaves open the possibility that unbelieving Jews will join the full
celebration of Israel's redemption later on in Stage Four, *after* Jewish
and Gentile Christians have inaugurated the feasting with "Abraham
and Isaac and Jacob and all the prophets" (13:28).

This scenario meshes well with Luke's insistence elsewhere that
Jesus and the church are bringing about the fulfillment of empirical
Israel's hope (Acts 26:6–7; 28:19–20). It also fits with a word of Jesus
from the cross which occurs only in the Third Gospel: "Father,
forgive them; for they know not what they do" (Lk. 23:34; compare
also Stephen's dying words in Acts 7:60). Luke wants all Jews to find
their salvation within the house of Israel (Lk. 19:9–11).[13] Thus he
adds a cryptic promise to an otherwise doleful word of Jesus concerning Israel's rejection of his ministry:

> O Jerusalem, Jerusalem, killing the prophets and stoning those who are
> sent to you! How often would I have gathered your children together as
> a hen gathers her brood under her wings, and you would not! Behold, your
> house is forsaken. And I tell you, you will not see me until you say,
> "Blessed is he who comes in the name of the Lord!" (Lk. 13:34–35)

The last words quoted above might be read as a reference to Jesus'
triumphal entry into Jerusalem (Lk. 19:37–40). But that would be a
mistake. Luke's version of the entry, in contrast to Mt. 21:9 and Mk.
11:9–10, has carefully restricted all exclamations of blessing to Jesus'
Galilean disciples. According to the Third Gospel, no one from
Jerusalem greets the Nazarene prophet joyously. Quite the contrary.
In a passage distinctive to his Gospel, Luke reports that "when [Jesus]
drew near and saw the city he wept over it, saying, 'Would that even
today you knew the things that make for peace! But now they are hid
from your eyes' " (19:41–42). Luke wishes to show that the Jerusalemites cannot "see" Jesus' true significance as he enters Jerusalem
on his way to the cross. But this means that the prophecy recorded
in Lk. 13:35 must look forward to some *other* future event. This other
is probably Jesus' Parousia descent to Jerusalem as Son of Man
Messiah in the Kingdom of God (Lk. 21:27; Acts 1:11). Only then
will inhabitants of the city "see" that Jesus "comes in the name of

the Lord" for their redemption. Then belief in him will no longer be necessary. On that day Jerusalemites will repent of their blindness and welcome Jesus with blessings. Thereafter, the final restoration of Israel can proceed, even if many Jews must wait outside the banquet hall for a time.

Luke may be thinking of this temporary exclusion from God's eschatological feast in the parable of the prodigal son, unique to his Gospel. There we read that when the elder brother (symbolic of Jesus' Pharisaic listeners according to Lk. 15:1–2) learned of the great welcome meal prepared for his irresponsible younger brother (sinners who come to Jesus for forgiveness), "he was angry and refused to go in," even when his father entreated him to do so (15:28–30). As in 13:23–30 and 14:1–24, Luke suggests that some Jews are depriving themselves of joy by turning down God's invitations in the ministry of Jesus. Yet the parable does not end on a note of alienation. Instead, the father assures his firstborn: "Son, you are always with me, and all that is mine is yours" (15:31). An eternal promise hovers over this son, whether or not he decides to take part in the banquet honoring his younger brother. By analogy, the Fourth Stage of salvation history anticipated by Luke probably allows for unbelieving Israel to take possession of all that God has promised her, once Christians have tasted the firstfruits of the eschatological meal and "the times of the Gentiles" have come to an end (21:24). "Some are last who will be first, and some are first who will be last" (13:30).

If this interpretation accurately reflects Luke's thinking about the future of Israel, then we must take care not to read the last words he ascribes to Paul in Acts as God's rejection of the Jewish people (Acts 28:25–29). This passage, at the end of Luke's second volume, shows Paul invoking Is. 6:9–10 in a speech to the Jewish leaders at Rome:

> The Holy Spirit was right in saying to your fathers through Isaiah the prophet:
> "Go to this people, and say,
> You shall indeed hear but never understand,
> and you shall indeed see but never perceive.

> For this people's heart has grown dull,
> and their ears are heavy of hearing,
> and their eyes they have closed;
> lest they should perceive with their eyes,
> and hear with their ears,
> and understand with their heart,
> and turn for me to heal them."
> Let it be known to you then that this salvation of God has been sent to
> the Gentiles; they will listen. (Acts 28:25–28)

These verses are often cited as evidence that Luke has not only given
up on a Christian mission to Jews but has also pronounced unbelieving Jews altogether without hope of attaining God's salvation. However, it is probable, if our previous exegesis is correct, that Luke
understands the blindness of unbelieving Israel much as Paul does in
Romans 11: it is a temporary stage in salvation history which provides
special opportunity for the Gentiles. Eric Franklin's comments on
the conclusion of Acts are instructive:

> The final episode at Rome is to be understood as a justification of Chris-
> tianity in spite of its refusal by the Jews rather than as a turning aside from
> them. Paul's work among the Jews at Rome is not a total failure (28:24).
> Jewish disbelief is denounced in terms of Isaiah 6, which makes even their
> rejection of Christianity the outcome of prophecy, so giving further proof
> that it is not a falsification of the Christian claims. Nevertheless, Chris-
> tianity is still put forward as the "hope of Israel" (28:20), a designation
> that suggests that even now the Jews are unlikely to be abandoned. Paul
> announces the Gentile mission: "Let it be known to you that this salvation
> of God has been sent to the Gentiles; they will listen" (28:28). This is less
> a programme for the future than a justification of what has happened,
> where the Gentile mission and their response is used to contrast their
> attitude with that of the Jews and so to witness to the truth of the
> proclamation. As such, Paul's final statement is not a rejection of the Jews.
> Rather it is a commentary in the light of Scripture upon a situation which
> has arisen out of the Jewish refusal of the gospel and its ready acceptance
> by the Gentiles. . . . The priority of the Jews remains; their refusal presents
> a problem which cannot be solved by its dismissal but which can be
> approached in the light of Paul's address to Agrippa: "To this day I have
> had the help which comes from God, and so I stand here, testifying both

to small and great, saying nothing but what the prophets and Moses said would come to pass; that the Christ must suffer, and that, by being the first to rise from the dead, he would proclaim light both to the people [Israel] and to the Gentiles" (Acts 26:22–23). Paul's final journey does not cause the abandoning of that standpoint.[14]

Franklin seems to be right in his conclusion. Luke's fixation on Israel's "blindness" (already well established in Lk. 8:9–10; 10:21–22; 19:39–44; 23:34) represents not a final decision about the future of the Jewish people but an attempt to explain why most Jews do not accept their own Messiah. Like Paul in Romans 9–11, Luke alternates between blaming the Jews for their unbelief (Acts 7:51–52; 13:46) and, more often, identifying it as a necessary phase in God's plan (Acts 3:17–18; 4:27–28; 13:27–29; 28:26–27). Like Paul, the third Evangelist believes that God's mercy will bless Abraham's posterity forever (Lk. 1:54–55).

Here it may be wise to remind ourselves that Luke is a fallible human being. For all his open-mindedness regarding the final fate of the Jews, he is not simply brimful of positive feelings toward them. Like Matthew, he frequently sees Jews as opponents, especially the Jewish rulers (Lk. 23:35; Acts 4:11; 5:12–18, 27–32). Indeed, Luke sometimes slants his history of Jesus and the church so as to express hostility toward Jews. For example, Luke's passion story assigns more responsibility for Jesus' death to Jews and less to Pilate than Mark's does (contrast Mk. 15:1–20 with Lk. 23:1–25). Moreover, Luke's Stephen lays a heavy weight of guilt not only upon the Jerusalem council before which he is being tried, but also upon Jewish rulers in ages past (Acts 7:51–53). Again, Luke sometimes uses the undifferentiated phrase "the Jews" to denote those opposed to Jesus' gospel and its apostolic preachers (e.g., Acts 9:22f.; 12:3, 11; 17:5; 18:12; 20:3).[15] Finally, Luke's opinion that unbelieving Jews have forfeited their place at the messianic banquet for a time will certainly stick in the throats of practicing Jews today. This sobering evidence must be placed alongside the pro-Jewish attitudes expressed by Luke. We Christians dare not (and need not) whitewash our canonical authors. If Luke felt ambivalence toward his Jewish contemporaries, then it is our vocation today to determine what meaning that ancient double-mindedness holds for us in our relationships with modern Jews.

LUKE'S MODERATE CRITIQUE OF THE PHARISEES

A curious instance of Luke's ambivalence toward Jews and Judaism may be found in his distinctive treatment of the Pharisees. Like Matthew, Luke sometimes follows Mark's story line by presenting Jesus' opponents as Pharisees (e.g., Lk. 5:33–39//Mk. 2:18–22; Lk. 6:1–5//Mk. 2:23–28; Lk. 12:1//Mk. 8:15). On occasion, he even inserts them into controversies where Mark and Matthew do not have them (Lk. 5:17ff.; 7:29f.; 16:14; 17:20f.). The most famous of these innovations is the story of the Pharisee and the publican (18: 9–14). This account has often been taken by Christian interpreters as a virtual equation of Pharisaism with self-righteousness. But it is not so clear that this is Luke's intent. He introduces the story with an editorial comment that Jesus "told this parable to *some* who trusted in themselves that they were righteous and despised others" (18:9, italics added). To be sure, the Pharisee in this story does function as a symbol for the self-righteous. But apparently Luke does not think that Jesus told the parable against Pharisees as such, for they are not among his listeners in this narrative. The "some" of 18:9 may even refer to disciples (see 17:22ff.; 18:15). We move beyond the text when we suppose that Luke thinks *all* Pharisees are self-righteous.

In fact, Luke resists turning all Pharisees into enemies of the gospel. This is just what makes his picture of them so complex. In Lk. 6:2, for example, Jesus' opponents are characterized as "some of the Pharisees," a qualification which is unique to the third Evangelist's version of the grain-plucking incident. In another Lucan expansion of Mark's outline, "some Pharisees" (a friendlier group than the first) look out for Jesus' welfare by warning him of Herod's plot to kill him (13:31). For Luke, no Pharisee takes part in conspiracies to execute Jesus. Thus, while Mark (with Matthew following him) states that "the Pharisees went out, and immediately held counsel with the Herodians against [Jesus], how to destroy him" (Mk. 3:6//Mt. 12: 14), Luke's parallel version reads: "They were filled with fury and discussed with one another what they might do to Jesus" (Lk. 6:11). But the rest of Luke's Gospel says nothing about any concrete plans issuing from this discussion, which suggests that in his opinion the Pharisees decided not to urge Jesus' death. Their legendary moderation wins out over their "fury."

In Luke's view, it was "the chief priests and the scribes and the principal men of the people [who] sought to destroy him" (Lk. 19:47). Just a few verses earlier, Luke pictures "some of the Pharisees" taking offense at the proclamation of Jesus' disciples that he is "the King who comes in the name of the Lord!" (19:37–40). But these Pharisees are clearly not the plotters of 19:47. Surprisingly, 19:39 is the very last reference in Luke's Gospel to Pharisees. They play no role at all in the arrest, trial, or crucifixion of Jesus. Unlike Matthew, the third Evangelist refrains from building a polemic against Pharisees by means of Jesus' Temple speeches (see Mt. 21:45; 22:15–46; and ch. 23). Neither does he record Matthew's allegation that it was the Pharisees in league with the chief priests who petitioned Pilate for armed guards to secure Jesus' tomb (Mt. 27:62–66). Luke simply ignores Mark's assertion that the priests, scribes, and elders dispatched "some of the Pharisees and some of the Herodians, to entrap [Jesus] in his talk" (Mk. 12:13). Similarly, he drops from his narration at least three other hostile references to Pharisees found in the Marcan outline (Mk. 7:1ff.; 8:11–13; 10:2–9).

Unique to Luke's Gospel and instructive of his attitudes toward Judaism are stories about Jesus' table fellowship with Pharisees (Lk. 7:36–50; 11:37–54; 14:1–24). All three Synoptic Evangelists highlight Jesus' ministry at table to the common people, to the outcasts of Israel's society, and to his disciples. But only Luke tells us that Jesus also accepted dinner invitations from Pharisees. The inference is that some Pharisees were positively inclined toward Jesus and considered him ritually clean enough to share with them in the intimate act of eating. In each of the stories cited above, Jesus is portrayed as extremely critical of Pharisaic practices. In fact, the strongest denuncia-

tion of Pharisees delivered anywhere in the Lucan writings occurs
during one of these meals when Jesus tells his host:

> Now you Pharisees cleanse the outside of the cup and of the dish, but
> inside you are full of extortion and wickedness. You fools! Did not he who
> made the outside make the inside also? But give for alms those things
> which are within; and behold, everything is clean for you.
>
> But woe to you Pharisees! for you tithe mint and rue and every herb,
> and neglect justice and the love of God; these you ought to have done,
> without neglecting the others. Woe to you Pharisees! for you love the best
> seat in the synagogues and salutations in the market places. Woe to you!
> for you are like graves which are not seen, and men walk over them
> without knowing it. (Lk. 11:39–44)[16]

But even here, in these obviously angry words, the careful reader will
note that Jesus does not drum the Pharisees out of God's people or
dismiss them as incorrigible hypocrites. Although he accuses them of
not living up to the image of piety they project, he also gives them
counsel regarding the integration of ritual practice with justice and
love. In other words, Jesus rebukes his table partners like a teacher
or reformer, not a final judge. To them as well as to other Israelites,
he points out the door of repentance and new behavior.

We see this same didactic thrust in Lk. 7:36–50, where Jesus
attempts to instruct his Pharisaic host Simon in the profundities of
love and forgiveness. Jesus' critique of his host is ultimately a friendly
one designed to help rather than condemn ("Simon, I have something to say to you," 7:40). Luke 14:1–24 can also be understood in
this manner, as these verses show:

> [Jesus] said . . . to the [Pharisee] who had invited him, "When you give
> a dinner or a banquet, do not invite your friends or your brothers or your
> kinsmen or rich neighbors, lest they also invite you in return, and you be
> repaid. But when you give a feast, invite the poor, the maimed, the lame,
> the blind, and you will be blessed, because they cannot repay you. You will
> be repaid at the resurrection of the just." (Lk. 14:12–14)

This saying holds out a conditional promise. Indirectly, it reveals
Luke's hope that some Pharisees at least will heed Jesus' advice and
thereby receive commendation at the final resurrection. Despite his

words of criticism, Luke's Jesus shows himself kindly disposed toward these upright practitioners of Judaism. They must repent and change their ways, just as other Jews (and Gentiles) must, but their transformation is by no means impossible if they take Jesus' words to heart. It is noteworthy that no counsel of Jesus to the Pharisees in Luke urges them to accept him as Messiah. Instead, he exhorts them to live up to the Judaism which they profess.

In Acts, Luke's positive stance toward Pharisees becomes even more apparent. There he criticizes only one group of them: *Christian* Pharisees associated with the Jerusalem church who insist that Gentile believers must submit to circumcision (Acts 15:5ff.). Throughout his second volume, Luke takes an altogether amiable attitude toward unbelieving Pharisees. He consistently portrays them as a moderate element in Judaism that opposes the persecution of the church. This attitude is communicated most graphically in Luke's depiction of the Pharisaic leader Gamaliel, grandson of Hillel and "a teacher of the law, held in honor by all the people" (5:34). Gamaliel urges the Jerusalem council to let Christian leaders alone while adopting a wait-and-see policy toward the church, "for if this plan or this undertaking is of men, it will fail; but if it is of God, you will not be able to overthrow them. You might even be found opposing God!" (5:38f.). Luke's generous portrait of Gamaliel is especially significant because the Pharisaic leaders at Jamnia in his own day traced their lineage back through this man.

Most striking to modern Christian readers, perhaps, is Luke's repeated assertion in Acts that Paul remained a practicing Pharisee to the end of his ministry. Luke's Paul claims to have learned the law from Gamaliel (Acts 22:3) and never to have departed from the Pharisaic understanding of it (23:6; 24:14f.; 25:8; 26:5; 28:17). At his hearing before a Jerusalem council, Paul uses his party affiliation to good advantage:

> When Paul perceived that one part were Sadducees and the other Pharisees, he cried out in the council, "Brethren, I am a Pharisee, a son of Pharisees; with respect to the hope and the resurrection of the dead I am on trial." And when he had said this, a dissension arose between the

Pharisees and the Sadducees; and the assembly was divided. For the Sadducees say that there is no resurrection, nor angel, nor spirit; but the Pharisees acknowledge them all. Then a great clamor arose; and some of the scribes of the Pharisees' party stood up and contended, "We find nothing wrong in this man. What if a spirit or an angel spoke to him?" (Acts 23:6–9)

Luke's account of this proceeding is surely more than a story about Paul's cleverness. Together with what Luke says elsewhere about Pharisees, we recognize it as another stone in the bridge he is building to connect the church with post-70 Judaism as he knows it. Christians, he argues, embody *the authentic understanding and practice of Pharisaic Judaism.* Judaism and the Christian movement are not two separate religions. Rather, Christ's church must be thought of as that "Way" which takes up the law, the prophets, and the traditions of Judaism into itself and obeys them fully (Acts 24:14; 28:17–20). Luke and some of his readers may be experiencing the official split between church and synagogue which began to take effect in the late 80s (see Lk. 6:22f.). But if this is so, surprisingly little is made of it.

CONCLUSIONS

The sum of the evidence we have examined indicates that one of Luke's major objectives in his two-volume work is to locate Jesus and the church securely within *Israel's history.* Jesus and the church do not supersede that history or replace it. Nor do they render Israel's ancient hopes obsolete. We Christians may speak of the events narrated in Luke-Acts as "fulfillments" of the Hebrew Scripture (Lk. 4:21; 24:44; Acts 1:16; 3:18; 28:25), but if we want to take Luke seriously, our use of this word cannot imply that unbelieving Jews lose their place in Israel's history and the saving plan of God. For Luke, fulfillment happens in four stages, the last of which represents a Jewish renaissance.

What intentions lie behind Luke's effort to underscore the Jewish character of Jesus and the church? Jervell has argued that in Acts Luke writes to Jewish Christians who are suspicious of Paul on grounds that he has taught Jewish believers not to obey the law, especially circumcision (Acts 21:20f.). In Jervell's view, Acts is an apology for Paul designed to convince Jewish-Christian readers that the apostle was altogether orthodox. This knowledge would enable them both to accept Paul themselves and also to answer the critiques leveled against Paul by their unbelieving Jewish neighbors.[17] But Jervell's hypothesis seems inadequate. On the grounds of internal evidence alone, it is improbable that Acts was written primarily to *Jewish* Christians. They would hardly need to be instructed about the difference between Sadducees and Pharisees, as Luke's readers are in Acts 23:8.[18] Even if Luke writes through Theophilus to the church as a whole, this, by the 80s, would be predominantly Gentile.

We now have sufficient data to construct a profile of Luke's typical readers. As Gentile Christians who lived some years after Jerusalem's destruction, they would be neither well informed about pre-70 Judaism, nor well disposed toward the Judaism of their own day.[19] The Jesus of Luke's Gentile readers would be a relatively de-Judaized heavenly Lord. To the degree that they knew Paul, they would honor him as the virtually non-Jewish founder of their own Gentile congregations. Within these readers Luke is attempting to produce a monumental change of consciousness. Throughout his two-volume work he steadfastly locates Jesus and the church (especially Paul) in Israel's history for the purpose of calling his Gentile Christian addressees back to their Jewish roots.[20] For Luke, a large part of the Gospel's "reliability" (Lk. 1:4) resides in its ongoing continuity with Israel, and it is just this that he wants his readers to understand. The church does not replace empirical Israel as God's people, even though it now functions as the red thread or "Way" which leads most surely to the fulfillment of Israel's hope.

It appears, then, that Luke writes, at least in part, to correct the attitudes of his Gentile readers regarding their connections with Israel. He even risks pronouncing them "associate" members of God's people, junior partners with God's original chosen ones (Acts 15:16–18).[21] Perhaps Luke is trying to reestablish the influence of Jewish Christians, clearly on the wane in the Gentile church of his day. Supportive of this thesis is the fact that Jewish Christians are consistently presented in Acts as the early church's leaders.[22] Perhaps

Luke also wishes to defend Jewish Christians before Gentile Christians who, more and more, are coming to think of them as an anachronism. We modern Christian readers, who too often judge Judaism itself obsolete, will find much to ponder in Luke's "Israelization" of Jesus and the church.

CHAPTER 6

John: A Painful Break with Judaism

DECISION AT JAMNIA
AND THE GOSPEL WRITER'S RESPONSE

Sometime around the year 85 c.e. the rabbinic sages at Jamnia made a critical decision. They felt compelled to draw a sharp line between themselves and that element within the Christian church which wished to consider itself Jewish. This decision to institutionalize the separation of synagogue and church took a form that was consistent with the pacifism of the rabbis. No persecutions were ordered. No edict prohibited Christians from attending synagogue services. Rather, a change was introduced into one of the chief synagogue prayers, the so-called Eighteen Benedictions. The twelfth benediction was altered so as to include Christians and other groups deemed heretical in a curse. Apparently, the theory was that wherever this new version of the Benedictions was prayed, Jewish Christians could not in good conscience participate. If a local synagogue ruler had some doubt about whether a man taking part in the service was actually praying the curse, he could have the person called up before the Torah niche to *lead* the prayer as a "delegate of the congregation." Thus the rabbis created an effective means of forcing Jewish Christians to face their convictions and decide either for or against fellowship with the synagogue.[1]

We do not know how the action taken at Jamnia was received by the various synagogues scattered throughout the ancient world. Presumably, the new prayer found acceptance most speedily in Palestine and Syria, where the rabbinic academy wielded its greatest power. But we have no record of any resistance from Hellenistic synagogues. By the beginning of the second century it is clear that Judaism and the church had pretty much gone their separate ways. Certain portions of the Fourth Gospel probably came into existence shortly after the synagogues and churches located in its area had parted company.

THE FOURTH GOSPEL: A LAYERED DOCUMENT

According to Raymond E. Brown, the composition of what we now call John's Gospel went through five distinguishable stages:

1. The "raw material" for the Gospel consisted of traditions about the words and works of Jesus. In form this material was like that which grew into the Synoptic tradition, but in content it often differed. Some of this early material, particularly the historical reminiscences, originated in eyewitness accounts from John, the son of Zebedee.

2. The material then developed for several decades along specific patterns as it was transmitted through oral preaching and teaching. According to Brown, a Johannine school, i.e., a group of John's disciples, was responsible for this stage. One chief disciple, especially gifted with theological insight and dramatic skill, shaped the body of tradition into a unified story. This person was also the leading light in stages 3 and 4.

3. The tradition was published for the first time as a written document. The chief disciple now became the fourth Evangelist. Though the earliest tradition was transmitted in Aramaic, it had by this time passed into Greek, and so this first edition of the Gospel was a Greek document.

4. This stage represents a second edition by the Evangelist. One reason for its appearance was to speak to the difficulties of Jewish Christians who were being confronted in synagogues with the new version of the Eighteen Benedictions.

5. A final edition, under the direction of someone other than the Evangelist, appeared late in the first century. Probably this redactor was a close friend or disciple of the Evangelist. He is responsible for

the addition of duplicate discourses, alongside those appearing in the edition he received, especially in chs. 3, 6, and 12. He also seems to have introduced most of that large body of material which we now call the farewell discourses (chs. 14–17).[2]

Not all New Testament scholars agree with Brown's version of the Fourth Gospel's history. Some find insufficient evidence for positing so many stages of development. Others feel unable to reconstruct the stages with such confidence. Yet nearly all scholars currently hold to some version of the view that the book's composition took place over a relatively long period of time. It now seems clear that John's Gospel presents us with very early material about the ministry of Jesus not found in the Synoptic writings.[3] On the other hand, it also contains material which best fits that time when the decision of the Jamnia sages began to take effect in Judaism, between 85 and 100 C.E. Throughout the Gospel, however, we find evidence that the Johannine church wished to consider itself Jewish. To this evidence we now turn.

The fourth Evangelist shows a special interest in relating Jesus' ministry to the chief Jewish feasts. In contrast to the Synoptic accounts, he explicitly states that Jesus cleansed the Temple early in his ministry *during the Passover holidays* (Jn. 2:13–23). John 4:45 is probably a second reference to this Passover cleansing: "So when he came to Galilee, the Galileans welcomed him, having seen all that he had done in Jerusalem at the feast, for they too had gone to the feast." In addition, the Johannine Jesus delivers his "bread of life" discourse in the synagogue of Capernaum just prior to the Passover season (6:24–59). In harmony with the Synoptic Gospels, Jesus' last days in Jerusalem are said to take place during Passover (11:55ff.). But over against the Synoptics, John highlights this climactic Passover by devoting eight entire chapters to it. Unique to the fourth Evangelist is a major speech by Jesus at the Feast of Tabernacles, the setting for which is Herod's Temple (7:1–43). During the Feast of Dedication, Jesus is once again pictured in the Temple; on this occasion he answers questions in the portico of Solomon (10:22ff.). The "feast of the Jews" referred to in 5:1 is uncertain. But if 4:45 describes Passover, then sequentially the next major festival period would be Pentecost.

These details present significant data about the Fourth Gospel because they are so distinctive. Matthew, Mark, and Luke mention only one Jewish feast, Passover, and then only in connection with the passion narrative. The fourth Evangelist clearly thinks that Jewish feasts have something to do with the proper understanding of Jesus' ministry. But what? Does he merely wish to assure his readers that Jesus was a pious, observant Jew who went up to Jerusalem even more often than tradition recommended? That seems unlikely, for elsewhere the Evangelist presents Jesus as one who stands over against the popular piety of his brother-sister Jews (2:14–21; 4:21–24; 5:8–11, 15–18, 37–47; 8:39–47, 56–58; 10:7–8). In all probability, the connection between Jesus' teaching in the synagogue or Temple and three (or four) of the Jewish festivals was meant to help John's readers understand their own Jewish heritage in a new way. By placing some of Jesus' self-disclosure speeches in the context of Judaism's traditional festivals, the Evangelist effects a reinterpretation of the liturgical calendar. In his view, believers must now incorporate Jesus' words into their festival orders of worship, right alongside the customary readings from Torah.[4] It is Jesus who offers the decisive interpretive key to the meaning of their ancient worship traditions.

This attempt by the Evangelist to combine old and new makes most sense if he is writing to Christians who wish to maintain membership in both church and synagogue. These would be Jewish Christians who reject the rabbinic charge that their confession of Jesus' Messiahship disqualifies them from the worshiping people of Israel. Perhaps the Fourth Gospel's emphasis on Jesus' relationship to Jewish feasts arose about the time members of John's congregation began to feel unwelcome in the synagogues, perhaps even earlier. True to its deep Jewish roots, the Johannine church continued to revere the ancient feasts, now albeit with a new messianic slant. Whether the community actually observed these feasts after its separation from the synagogue we cannot tell. But the need to speak about them and link them with the new life in Christ persisted. And so this reflective material found its place in the final edition of the Gospel.

JOHN'S TWO-LEVEL APPROACH

Here we are operating with some presuppositions about the Fourth Gospel which ought to be spelled out more precisely. We are assuming that the Evangelist has shaped Christian traditions which he inherited (whether in oral or written form) into an account of Jesus' ministry designed specifically for the church of his day. This means that the words and acts of Jesus must be understood on two levels. On one level, they are events in the historical ministry of Jesus. They happened once, long ago—even for the Evangelist and his readers. On another level, however, these events are still happening. They are taking place within the Johannine congregation. Through the Spirit, the written text of John's Gospel allows the risen Christ to speak and act not just "then," in the presence of his first disciples and the Jews contemporary with him, but also "now," in direct response to the needs of Jewish-Christian readers in the late first century. (See 14:25f.; 15:26; 16:7–15.)

This "two-level drama"[5] may be perceived in John 9. The story related there concerns Jesus' healing of a man blind since birth. Some of the Pharisees object that this healing cannot be from God because Jesus performed it on the Sabbath. A dispute follows. All of this could have happened, and perhaps did happen, in the ministry of Jesus. But then the story takes an unusual turn. The parents of the man born blind are interrogated by synagogue officials. The frightened parents play dumb, for as the Gospel writer tells us: "The Jews had already agreed that if any one should confess him to be Christ, he was to be put out of the synagogue" (9:22). Later, the man himself is questioned and, in fact, he does suffer expulsion from the synagogue fellowship (9:24–34).

In 9:22 the RSV phrase "put out of the synagogue" is expressed by a single Greek word, *aposynagōgos*. This seems to be a technical term meaning something like "excommunication," and except for Jn. 12:42 and 16:2 it occurs nowhere else in the New Testament. John 9:22 and its parallels will surprise us if we remember that Jesus' earliest disciples in the Jerusalem church, who surely confessed Jesus as the Christ, never found themselves excluded from either synagogue or Temple. Nor does Paul indicate in his letters that he ever fell under such a synagogue ban. Most likely, 9:22 reflects a time in the church's history when the decision reached at Jamnia was coming into general practice at the local synagogue level. The "excommunication" (for so it is seen by the Evangelist and his readers) is transposed by John into an event that occurs "back then" in the ministry of the historical Jesus; but actually it is first happening "now" in the Johannine congregation, perhaps as the direct result of a healing accomplished through some Jewish believer who insisted on giving all credit to Jesus the Christ.[6] Such is the two-level drama: A word or deed of Jesus in the past is given new shape by the experience of John's community late in the first century.

This hypothesis finds added support in 16:2, where Jesus, speaking to his disciples, foretells a time when "they will put you out of the synagogues [literally: "they will make you into people outside the synagogue" *(aposynagōgous)*]; indeed, the hour is coming when whoever kills you will think he is offering service to God." Here the synagogue excommunication is predicted as if it did not, after all, happen in the ministry of Jesus, but is rather altogether future. Moreover, the killing of Christians, presumably at the hands of Jews, is also foretold.[7] This may be a reference to the deaths of Stephen and James the brother of John (Acts 7:54ff.; 12:1f.), but since the second person plural "you" is used, we should probably suspect that the killings are recent events known to the Johannine congregation in a more personal way. Let us note, by the way, that John does not lay these executions at the feet of synagogue officials; they may have resembled the mob action that led to Stephen's demise.

In 12:42 we encounter another version of the two-level drama. There the Evangelist states that "many even of the authorities believed in him [Jesus], but for fear of the Pharisees they did not confess it, lest they should be put out of the synagogue *(aposynagōgoi)*." Who are these authorities who believed in Jesus? The Greek word is *archōn* and could refer to the local ruler of a synagogue or a member of the Jerusalem Sanhedrin. In neither case does the assertion make much sense within the ministry of the historical Jesus, for prior to 70 C.E. the Pharisees, as a group, would not have held sufficient political power to exclude such an *archōn* from his office, at least not on the sole ground of his confessing Jesus to be the Christ. But if we read the text as a message intended for the Johannine church late in the first century, it makes a good deal of sense. By then, the Pharisees at Jamnia did exercise considerable authority and presumably could have forced a Christian synagogue ruler to lead his congregation in praying the revised version of the Eighteen Benedictions.[8]

JOHN'S POLEMIC AGAINST JEWS AND JUDAISM

What has the evidence shown us so far? The Evangelist's effort to link speeches of Jesus with the Jewish festivals strongly suggests that these festivals held an important place in the religious life of his readers. It was their wish somehow to retain the fundamentals of Jewish worship. But 9:22, 12:42, and 16:2 show that dual citizenship in synagogue and church, and traditional worship along with it, had become impossible. The Jamnia academy, under pressure of various sorts, had defined the relationship between Jews and Christians in either-or terms. The Christian community behind the Fourth Gospel felt both grief and anger at the enforcement of the Jamnia decision. Through its spokesman, the Evangelist, it reacted with a series of theological rebuttals that have crippled Jewish-Christian relations ever since.

Let us examine the passages that have come to be most offensive to Jews. Those texts which reflect the high Christology of the Fourth Gospel will provide a good starting point. For example, in John's Prologue, Christ becomes the Word who was ever with God. Indeed, as the Word, he *is* God, and through him all things have come into being (1:1–3). This Word became flesh in the person of Jesus (1:14). Throughout his earthly incarnation Jesus is fully divine. He tells his disciple Philip, "He who has seen me has seen the Father" (14:9). He insists, in a clear allusion to Ex. 3:14, "Before Abraham was, I am" (8:58). Furthermore, there are predicates to this "I am." "I am the door" (10:9). "I am the way, and the truth, and the life" (14:6). "I am the true vine" (15:1). After the resurrection Jesus' doubting disciple Thomas touches his wounds and exclaims, "My Lord and my God!" (20:28). These are lofty claims, and they appear only in the Fourth Gospel. Observant Jews of all ages must reject them on the ground that the Messiah they expect would never assume equality with the one God.

Yet ascriptions of divinity to Jesus, strange as they sound to Jewish ears, do not constitute the core difficulty in the Fourth Gospel for contemporary Jewish-Christian dialogue. The thorniest issue of all is the manner in which the Evangelist treats Jews and Judaism. In contrast to the Synoptic writers, the fourth Evangelist refers to Jesus' coreligionists in a strangely undifferentiated way. They are simply "the Jews" (see 2:18; 5:16ff.; 6:41, 52; 7:15; 8:52–59; 10:31; 18:36; 20:19). For the most part, we do not see Jesus (as the Synoptic Gospels picture him) disputing with the Pharisees, opposing the Sadducees, or contradicting the scribes. Instead, he simply stands over against "the Jews." This phrase "the Jews" becomes a shibboleth which usually means nothing other than "unbelievers" and "enemies of God." Not a faction of the priestly rulers, but "the Jews" are blamed for trying to kill Jesus (5:16ff.). Sadly, the Evangelist's choice of this comprehensive term encourages his readers to separate themselves and Jesus from the whole Jewish nation. This separation is already implicit in the Prologue when the writer states: "He [Jesus] came to his own home, and his own people received him not" (1:11).

But the Evangelist draws a further, more extreme conclusion from the Jewish opposition to Jesus. Not only have "the Jews" rejected Jesus, they have also rejected God. And in so doing they have forfeited their status as God's chosen people. Their past counts for nothing now that Jesus has come. This theme emerges throughout the Gospel, as the following chain of passages will demonstrate. In examining them, Christian readers may find it useful to imagine themselves in the place of a modern Jew:

The law was given through Moses; grace and truth came through Jesus Christ. (Jn. 1:17)

Truly, truly, I say to you, unless one is born of water and the Spirit, he cannot enter the kingdom of God (3:5). He who believes in [the Son] is not condemned; he who does not believe is condemned already, because he has not believed in the only Son of God. (Jn. 3:18)

[The Father's] voice you [Jews] have never heard, his form you have never seen; and you do not have his word abiding in you, for you do not believe him whom he has sent. . . . I know that you have not the love of God within you. . . . Do not think that I shall accuse you to the Father; it is Moses who accuses you, on whom you set your hope. (Jn. 5:37–45)

[The Jews] answered him, "Abraham is our father." Jesus said to them, "If you were Abraham's children, you would do what Abraham did, but now you seek to kill me, a man who has told you the truth which I heard from God; this is not what Abraham did. You do what your father did." They said to him, "We were not born of fornication; we have one Father, even God." Jesus said to them, "If God were your Father, you would love me, for I proceeded and came forth from God. . . . Why do you not understand what I say? It is because you cannot bear to hear my word. You are of your father the devil, and your will is to do your father's desires. . . . He who is of God hears the words of God; the reason why you do not hear them is that you are not of God." (Jn. 8:39–47)

So Jesus again said to them, "Truly, truly, I say to you, I am the door of the sheep. All who came before me are thieves and robbers; but the sheep did not heed them" (10:7–8).

I am the way, and the truth, and the life; no one comes to the Father, but by me. If you had known me, you would have known my Father also. (Jn. 14:6–7)

He who hates me hates my Father also. If I had not done among them the works which no one else did, they would not have sin; but now they have seen and hated both me and my Father. It is to fulfil the word that is written in their law, "They hated me without a cause." (Jn. 15:23–25)

It is hoped that we Christians have not become so hardened or apathetic that we find ourselves incapable of sharing the anguish experienced by Jews today when they read these words or hear them read as Scripture in Christian churches. Whatever theologians may make of them, these texts (unique to the Fourth Gospel) certainly suggest that with the coming of Jesus, Judaism and the Jewish people have lost all religious value. Indeed, according to the fourth Evangelist, Jews themselves bear full responsibility for this obsolescence! Here the Pauline paradox is dissolved. The apostle had said that Jews who could not accept Jesus were enemies of the Gospel. At the same time, however, he called them "beloved [of God] for the sake of their forefathers" (Rom. 11:28). In Paul's view, all Jews would eventually enjoy the fullness of God's mercy, regardless of their belief or disbelief (Rom. 11:25–32). In the Fourth Gospel this tension disappears. The dimension of depth evaporates, and because of this flatness Jews and Christians have suffered much in the ensuing centuries.

IS THE FOURTH GOSPEL ANTI-SEMITIC?

So the question arises: Is the Fourth Gospel properly classified as an anti-Semitic document? We must certainly admit that it has functioned that way. The crazed emotions that produced pogroms, inquisitions, and gas chambers, as well as the more subtle prejudices of our own day, have been partially fueled by the idea, so prevalent in our Gospel, that Jews and Judaism are passé. John proclaims the Jewish people and their religion outmoded. Yet they do not go away. They survive, and sometimes they prosper. They contribute great gifts to the humanization of the world. In all ages some Christians have taken offense at this Jewish presence. Such threatened believers have decided that in order to justify the fourth Evangelist's conclusions they must *make* the Jews go away through conversion, ostracism, and even extermination. Of course, it is absurd to hold John (and other New Testament writers who take similar positions) responsible for all Christian anti-Semitism. Nevertheless, as Christendom's most popular missionary book, the Fourth Gospel has played an unfortunate role in fitting out new converts with a ready-made prejudice against Jews. Moreover, its uncritical public reading as Scripture in Christian churches has fanned the embers of hatred deep in the psyches of otherwise moderate and tolerant parishioners. In short, the Fourth Gospel *becomes* anti-Semitic whenever it is read or taught in such a way as to suggest that our attitude toward Jews ought to be the same as the author's.

Is there some way to affirm the Fourth Gospel's place as Scripture of the church, while at the same time minimizing or eliminating the danger that it will cultivate prejudice against Jews? Can we endorse its proclamation of the good news, so dear to Christians, without canonizing its anti-Judaism? One way of moving toward an answer to these questions is to clarify even further the historical situation which produced the final version of the Gospel.

JOHN'S ALL-ENCOMPASSING CHRISTOLOGY

We have said that the Johannine church experienced anger and grief over its exclusion from the synagogue. Let us try to understand the relationship between these feelings and the theology of the Gospel. The Johannine church had tried to remain Jewish. That was no easy task in the last years of the first century. After 70, the church rapidly became a predominantly Gentile group. Increasingly, this church looked with disdain upon "unbelieving" Judaism and, in all probability, upon those Jews who tried to combine their practice of Judaism with Christian faith. It is hard to believe that the Johannine congregation got much encouragement from the church at large in its effort to maintain its old ties. The sharpest pain came when these Jewish believers found themselves excluded from their own synagogue. Now all efforts to retain their Jewish heritage were seen to be fruitless. The Johannine church had become, in a very real sense, a church without a home. It was not ready for absorption into the Gentile church. Yet, by official proclamation, it was no longer Jewish. What was it to do in this wasteland?

One thing the Johannine church did have was its Lord. It heard and believed the promise of Christ: "I will not leave you desolate; I will come to you" (Jn. 14:18). Interestingly, the word here translated "desolate" is *orphanous*. Cut off from Judaism and reluctant to assimilate with Gentiles, the Johannine church felt orphaned. Yet it believed the gospel. And the specific form which that gospel took was the good news that Jesus was providing a home for it in the midst of a strange, unfriendly world. Through the Fourth Gospel, Jesus spoke directly to the needs of his isolated Jewish church:

> All that the Father gives me will come to me; and him who comes to me
> I will not cast out. (Jn. 6:37)

> If a man loves me, he will keep my word, and my Father will love him,
> and we will come to him and make our home with him. (Jn. 14:23)

The well-known "many mansions" passage should probably be interpreted along these lines. In 14:1ff. the departing Jesus tells his disciples (level 1), and therefore the Johannine church (level 2):

> Let not your hearts be troubled; believe in God, believe also in me. In my
> Father's house are many rooms; if it were not so, would I have told you
> that I go to prepare a place for you? And when I go and prepare a place
> for you, I will come again and will take you to myself, that where I am
> you may be also. (Jn. 14:1–3)

It is not so important for our purposes to ask whether Jesus here refers
to a present place or a future one after death. In fact, this question
does not seem to have been terribly significant to the Johannine
writer, for he believed that he and his community were participating
in an eternal, heavenly life even during their exile (5:24; 6:47–58).
The vital truth which this church needed to know was that despite
its exclusion from familiar surroundings, it had a place, a home, a
heritage assured to it by its Lord.

From this assurance something else begins to develop in the
Fourth Gospel. In certain passages Jesus not only provides a place,
but he also becomes the *entrance* to that place or even the *place itself*.
In the Fourth Gospel we can speak of a "hospitality Christology."
Jesus is the access to safety and nurture. "I am the door; if any one
enters by me, he will be saved, and will go in and out and find
pasture" (10:9). Jesus is "the way, and the truth, and the life" (14:6).
To be with him, either traveling or at rest, is to be at home. "If a
man loves me, he will keep my word, and my Father will love him,
and we will come to him and make our home with him" (14:23). In
the final analysis, that home is understood as none other than Christ
himself:

> I am the true vine, and my Father is the vinedresser. . . . Abide in me,
> and I in you. . . . I am the vine, you are the branches. He who abides in

me, and I in him, he it is that bears much fruit, for apart from me you can do nothing. If a man does not abide in me, he is cast forth as a branch and withers; and the branches are gathered, thrown into the fire and burned. If you abide in me, and my words abide in you, ask whatever you will, and it shall be done for you. (Jn. 15:1–7)

The vine imagery reminds us of Is. 5:1–7, where Israel appears as a vineyard. There is nothing subtle about the Evangelist's intention here. What he means to say is that Jesus and his church constitute a *replacement* for Israel. Other New Testament writers move in the direction of this mutual exclusivism, but only John follows the path to its bitter end.[9] According to Paul, Gentile believers were grafted into a holy root, the benefits of God's ancient covenant with Israel (Rom. 11:16ff.). But in the Fourth Gospel, Jesus himself becomes the holy root and Christians are his true branches. Consistent with this thought is the Johannine claim that for Christian believers, the authentic temple is not a building in Jerusalem but Jesus' own body (Jn. 2:19ff.). To abide in him is to worship legitimately. The Johannine church finds itself cut off from its festivals, from its synagogue liturgy. But it can still worship, for as Jesus tells the Samaritan woman (and the Johannine church!):

Woman, believe me, the hour is coming when neither on this mountain [Mt. Gerizim] nor in Jerusalem will you worship the Father. You worship what you do not know; we worship what we know, for salvation is from the Jews. But the hour is coming, and now is, when the true worshipers will worship the Father in spirit and truth, for such the Father seeks to worship him. (Jn. 4:21–23)

Jesus resurrected and resident in his church through the Spirit becomes a temple for the true worship of the Father. He is the new holy place.

He is also the new Torah. Nowhere in the Fourth Gospel are believers advised to obey the law. Rather, they are urged to enact the commandments of Jesus (13:34; 15:7–11). "For the law was given through Moses; grace and truth came through Jesus Christ" (1:17). In short, what John offers his readers is the good news that Jesus himself more than makes up for all the practices and institutions of

Judaism which they have had to leave behind. This is a quasi-mystical notion, strange to our Western sensibilities. It is a personalizing, a Christologizing of the entire religious life. Ironically, only a Jewish writer, with his concern for the sanctification of everyday life, could bring about such a radical shift in the church's thinking about Jesus.

THE IMPLICATIONS OF JOHANNINE EXCLUSIVISM

The fourth Evangelist's all-encompassing Christology, helpful as it must have been for his congregation, nevertheless produced a potentially hostile side effect: total exclusivism. The enlarged Jesus of the Fourth Gospel became quite naturally the only possible truth. "I am the way, and the truth, and the life; no one comes to the Father, but by me" (14:6). We can properly discern a joyful note in the Evangelist's proclamation of this "one way" gospel. But we must hear other melodies as well, more melancholy in character. The Evangelist is writing to a disenfranchised community, a congregation which, though rich in Spirit, feels deprived of its Jewish heritage. The high Christology of the gospel has developed in part to fill up that emptiness. Now the excluded ones become the exclusive ones. As long as John's congregation could find its identity in the synagogue, especially at worship, it must have retained some sensitivity for Israel's special status before God. It must have seen itself as a saving remnant *within* Israel. But after that painful break it reacted by denying to unbelieving Jews even their divine election. Now the Jews were no longer sons and daughters of God or of Abraham, but children of the devil (8:44). Now only Christians could enter God's Kingdom, through baptism by water and the Spirit (3:5).

Down through the centuries Christians without number have found great strength in the majestic Christ of the Fourth Gospel. Large numbers have come to faith through John's powerful images. It would be profoundly wrong for us Christians to deny or denigrate the grace that has come to us via the pages of this book. Nevertheless, knowing what we do today about how the Christology of the Fourth Gospel unfolded, we must move (in the name of grace) toward working out a more adequate view of its authority in the church. Can we not accept the love of God through Jesus Christ without denying it to those who believe differently (see Rom. 11:28)? Do we really need to canonize the Jewish-Christian argument which had so much to do with the Gospel's final editing?

If our answers to the last two questions are yes and no respectively, we need to do some further pondering. It may be that we shall have to develop some criteria for distinguishing *levels of authority* within the Fourth Gospel. Perhaps we can use our knowledge of the other canonical writings to determine what is primary and what is peripheral in the good news about Jesus Christ as mediated by John. This would not mean changing the text of the Gospel, but rather changing ourselves by equipping ourselves with new eyes and ears. With such sensitivity we could, perhaps, acknowledge both the "blindness" of the Gospel writer over against his Jewish neighbors in the first century and the Light of the world which shines through all darkness (Jn. 1:5). How this view of Biblical authority might actually function in the practical life of a Christian congregation is a matter requiring much careful and compassionate thought. We shall consider some initial suggestions for dealing with it in the next chapter.

CHAPTER 7

Israel at the Heart of the Church

A SHORT REVIEW

We have discovered, perhaps to the surprise of some Christian readers, how Jewish Jesus and the New Testament writers are. To be sure, they are not all Jewish in the same way; and none of them agreed precisely with the ruling opinions of Judaism in his day. Of John, it might even be said that he has replaced Judaism with Christology. Nevertheless, it seems fair to assert that not a single one of our subjects ever quite wraps up his relationship with Israel, the chosen people of God. For all of them, that relationship continues to burn at the heart of their respective self-definitions. A review of our conclusions, chapter by chapter, will support these broad claims. Then we can proceed to test our chief hypothesis: namely, that the New Testament as a whole, when understood historically, offers more resources than obstacles to those who value Jewish-Christian dialogue today.

JESUS AND THE JERUSALEM CHURCH

Jesus was a Galilean *hasid,* or holy man. His behavior inevitably irritated the strict Judean teachers of his day, whether Pharisee or Sadducee. The resulting conflicts with these teachers over Torah interpretation and practice did not, however, signify a fundamental break between Jesus and Judaism. Insofar as Jewish religious leaders took a hand in bringing about Jesus' trial before Pilate (and the

Pharisees were largely innocent of this), they must have acted from a concern for the political stability of Palestine. There is little doubt that some leaders considered Jesus either a revolutionary agitator or an apocalyptic prophet who could be perceived by the common people as a messianic pretender.

For his part, Jesus renounced violence while urging the renewal of Judaism's traditions and institutions. He called upon all Jews to repent in the light of God's will, revealed in the Hebrew Scriptures and dawning on earth anew in his own preaching of the imminent Kingdom. As God's elect people, Jews would enjoy the firstfruits of this coming reign. During his last supper with the disciples Jesus interpreted his mission as a final ratification of God's ancient covenant with Israel (Mk. 14:22–24). Jesus predicted the destruction of Herod's Temple, but not as a judgment on the Jewish people as a whole. Our study has skirted the difficult question of whether the historical Jesus actually considered himself to be the Messiah. If he did, his intention was surely to be *Israel's* Messiah.

The first followers of Jesus experienced him alive three days after his death on the cross. This experience, plus a subsequent reception of the Holy Spirit, was understood as a commissioning by the Risen One (now called Lord and Christ) to continue his work among the Jewish people, especially in Jerusalem. The first church worshiped regularly in Herod's Temple, despite its belief that this would soon be destroyed. There is no evidence that Jerusalem believers disobeyed Torah regulations or even the prevailing Pharisaic traditions during these early days of the church's history. Gradually, however, the first community began to discover that uncircumcised Gentiles could receive the Spirit of Jesus and come to faith in him.

Jewish believers welcomed these outsiders into their extended family with mixed feelings (Acts 10). Their ambivalence was understandable. In this new Gentile element they correctly sensed a challenge to their conservative position on Torah. Now they had to decide whether they could sit at the Lord's table with *goyim*, many of whom disregarded the laws of *kashruth*. The Gentile Cornelius probably continued to reside in Caesarea after his conversion, but his very proximity to Jerusalem troubled Torah-strict Jewish Christians (Acts

11). In fact, conservative attitudes predominated in the first church
for a long time. Cornelius and his like were regarded as exceptions.
No inclination toward an organized mission to Gentiles developed
until Jewish Christians in Jerusalem had evangelized their brother
and sister Jews for more than a decade. Even then, the push into Asia
Minor came only through activity initiated by the mixed Jewish-
Gentile church of Antioch (Acts 13).

Among Jerusalem Christians, the Risen One's commissioning had
established a common belief that they must be first of all a saving
remnant *within Judaism.* Luke pictures the earliest church as a bearer
of good news for Jews. According to Acts, the community of believers
stirs up the messianic expectations of many in Jerusalem, yet without
inciting a political revolution. This picture must be substantially
accurate. Otherwise, the local authorities would not have permitted
a public Christian movement to continue there. Only Stephen, with
his direct attack upon the Temple and the integrity of the Sanhedrin,
provoked a general persecution of the mother church. But according
to Acts, Stephen's views were not representative of his community's.
Throughout its history, the Jerusalem church maintained a steadfast
interest in the careful observance of Torah by Christians (Acts 11:
1–3; 15:13–21; 16:4; Gal. 2:11–14), including Temple worship and
the circumcision of male children born to Jewish believers (Acts
21:17–26).

PAUL

The apostle to the Gentiles knows of no religion called Christianity. Rather, he writes about life "in Christ," a matrix of sensations,
convictions, and practices proceeding from a powerful experience of
the risen Lord and interpreted (often rabbinically) in the light of
Jewish Scripture and tradition. Characteristic of this new life was a
daily inner guidance by the Spirit of Christ which Paul took to be
operative in all believers. Central to the apostle's thinking was his
belief that Christ's resurrection had inaugurated a unique period in
world history: a tension-filled overlapping of the messianic age with
"this world" which would shortly climax in the Risen One's return

from heaven to establish the Kingdom of God on earth.

Special conditions obtained during this interim time between Christ's resurrection and return. For example, Gentiles could now receive God's righteousness through faith in Christ. "Christ is the end of the law for righteousness to everyone who believes" (Rom. 10:4; author's translation). Paul wanted his Jewish coreligionists to share in this end-time righteousness too, but during the course of his ministry he learned that most could not accept Jesus as Messiah. The apostle felt deep pain at Jewish resistance to Jesus, but he did not conclude from it that God had abandoned his elect people. Paul never called the church "Israel" or "new Israel." On the contrary, since Israel had been chosen by God as the bearer of his promises for all people, and since God always keeps his promises, Paul foresaw that "all Israel" would be saved through grace (Rom. 11:26). For a time, the apostle surmised, nonbelieving Jews in Israel must be "broken off" from the benefits of God's promise to Abraham which were now manifesting themselves in a New Creation characterized by the gifts and fruit of the Spirit (Rom. 11:13–24; Gal. 3:14). But these spiritual benefits, which Paul sometimes refers to collectively as "salvation," would come to Israel when Christ returned. It was Paul's eschatological world view which led him to conceive of Christ as the alternative to Torah for righteousness. Even so, he never quite pronounced the Torah obsolete or replaced by Christ. Not for Jews, at any rate. "Saved" Israel would include Jews who currently adhered to Torah (Rom. 4:16).

Paul's letters contain numerous passages hostile to (some) Jews and the Torah. But in Romans, taken by many scholars to be the latest of Paul's major writings, the apostle expresses himself more carefully on the place of Torah in God's plan of salvation. There he exhibits an unconditional loyalty to the Jewish people. A strong case can be made that Romans represents the most mature expression of Paul's thought regarding Jews and Judaism. His "solution" to the conflicted relationship between Israel and church can hardly be taken as normative in a literal sense by contemporary Christians. Nevertheless, it is of great significance for contemporary Jewish-Christian dialogue that in this prominent and polemical apostle to the Gentiles a hope for reconciliation between Israel and the church triumphs over feelings of hostility.

MARK

This Evangelist is a Christian of Semitic (possibly Jewish) origin. He writes to Gentile believers who have probably undergone recent persecution at the hands of the Roman government, perhaps under Nero in 64. One of Mark's central purposes is to help his readers accept the fact that their sufferings will continue and even intensify because the cross remains a core element of discipleship to Jesus. As suffering servant–missionaries, Mark's readers dare not fall victim to false expectations. The siege of Jerusalem now commencing will not issue in Jesus' immediate return to vindicate his followers (Mk. 13: 14–27). For Mark, the tragic events unfolding in Palestine are part of God's larger, long-range plan to evangelize the entire world (13: 9–10, 34). One finds no evidence in this New Testament book that the Jewish-Roman war of 66–70 is understood by Christians as a judgment upon Jews for the execution of Jesus.

Mark addresses his Gentile readers by means of a "gospel," probably the first of this literary genre to appear in Christian circles. Mark's gospel mode of communication is an attempt to transmit a contemporary message to his readers by telling them a story about Jesus' earthly ministry, already more than three decades old. Mark's is a Jewish story in the sense that Jesus' ministry affirms the traditions and hopes of Israel. The one major exception is Jesus' opposition in Mark to the laws of *kashruth* (7:14–23). Here the Evangelist reflects a tradition that he may have learned in the mixed Jewish-Gentile churches of his day. It is probably incorrect to trace this position back to the historical Jesus. In other respects, Mark's Jesus stands well within Judaism. His mission is to bring about the renewal of Israel, thus ensuring its readiness for God's impending Kingdom. On the very night of his arrest in Jerusalem, Jesus dedicates his body and blood to a final affirmation of God's ancient convenant with Israel (14:22–25).

To be sure, Mark pictures Jesus as one misunderstood or rejected by most of his brother-sister Jews, including his family and disciples. But this picture of the "secret" Messiah (which Mark probably inherited from earlier Christian tradition and elaborated upon) represents not so much a judgment on the Jewish people as an explanation to Christians for Israel's resistance to Jesus' royal identity (4:10–12; 6:4–6). Mark's portrait of Jesus as lonely sufferer also encourages his readers in the midst of their own persecution by society and family (13:9–13).

Mark records many controversy stories involving Jesus and the Pharisees. For the most part, these are disputes about Torah interpretation and practice which do not issue in attempts to execute Jesus. No blanket condemnation of Pharisees can be perceived—only Matthew and Luke record "woes" against them. A few Pharisees are implicated by Mark in plots against Jesus (3:6; 12:13), but chief priests, scribes, elders, and the Roman procurator Pilate (along with people under their influence) are seen as the real forces behind his execution. In Mark's view, most of Jerusalem's inhabitants heard Jesus gladly (11:7–10, 18; 12:12, 37; 14:2). Only those "stirred up" into a lynch mob by the chief priests demanded his crucifixion (15: 10–15). At the moment of Jesus' death, "the curtain of the temple was torn in two." For Mark, this signifies not the demise of Judaism but the opening up of its treasures to Gentiles through Jesus' sacrifice (15:37–39). It is hard to imagine that Gentile Christians in the late 60s would conclude from Mark's Gospel that they were Israel's replacement.

MATTHEW

Like Mark, whose Gospel he seems to know, Matthew comes from a Semitic background. Indeed, he is almost certainly a *Jewish* Christian. Unlike Mark, he writes primarily to Jewish believers and demonstrates a fair knowledge of the methods used by first-century rabbis to interpret Scripture. Matthew's foremost concern is to picture Jesus as the perfect fulfillment of the Mosaic Torah (see esp. Mt. 5:17–19). This he does for the purpose of helping his readers defend themselves in disputes with their brother-sister Jews over Jesus' messianic identity. Matthew affirms the Christian mission to Gentiles but makes it clear that all converts must adhere to the Torah as interpreted by Jesus (28:19–20). According to their own self-understanding, Matthew and his community remain altogether Jewish. In fact, they regard themselves as the Jews who best know and do God's will. For them, the rabbinic leaders of the post-70 era hold only a limited authority (23:1–4).

Writing sometime after the Jewish-Roman war, Matthew adds to his parable of the royal marriage feast an excursus that seems to portray Jerusalem's destruction as a judgment upon Jews for failing to accept Jesus' message (22:7). But a close reading of this passage reveals that only those Jews who have mistreated the king's servants (Christians) and killed them are held responsible for the Holy City's demise (22:5–6; see also 23:34). In other words, Matthew distinguishes between the Jewish people in general and those Jews who have actively persecuted believers. Like Mark, Matthew denounces the chief priests and elders as primary agents in bringing about Jesus' death (27:20). In Matthew, however, Pilate's guilt diminishes (27: 18–19, 24), and the Pharisees receive extremely harsh criticism (esp. ch. 23)—far beyond anything that occurred in the ministry of the historical Jesus. Almost certainly, this heightened polemic against Pharisees reflects mounting conflict between Matthew's readers and the Jamnia Pharisees (or their supporters) who are attempting to purge Judaism of apocalyptic excesses after the 66–70 war. These post-70 disputes are read back into the days of Jesus. One finds no hard evidence, however, that Matthew and his community are actually suffering expulsion from the synagogues (see 23:1–3).

Matthew supports attempts to try to convince the Jewish people of Jesus' Messiahship (10:23), although he nowhere predicts that large numbers of them will become Christians. In 7:14 he suggests that the combined total of true believers from all nations will be small. There are hints that Matthew allows for an inheritance of God's Kingdom by nonbelieving Jews through acts of loving-kindness (7:21–27; 10:40–42; 25:31–46). On the other hand, those who *expect* to enjoy the bliss of the Kingdom by virtue of their Jewish origin ("the sons of the kingdom") will suffer exclusion from the messianic banquet and exile to "outer darkness" (8:11–12; see also 3:7–10). It is hard to tell whether the Evangelist identifies these "sons of the kingdom" with the Jewish leaders, or whether their number includes common people as well.

Crucial to Matthew's understanding of the gospel is his expectation that the risen Christ will return from heaven to establish God's Kingdom on earth within the present generation (16:28; 24:34). As the Evangelist writes, Jewish Christians are probably being viewed with suspicion by the Jamnia leadership and its supporters. But Matthew thinks that in a very short time the Kingdom will be "given to a nation producing the fruits of it" (21:43), presumably the church and those Jews who do God's will. At Jesus' return (but not before), his Jewish-Christian disciples will "sit on twelve thrones, judging the twelve tribes of Israel" (19:28). For Matthew, the church is not Israel's replacement. Instead, it is that group within Judaism which correctly perceives and expounds God's covenant with Israel.

LUKE-ACTS

In this complex two-volume work Luke attempts to anchor Jesus and the Christian movement solidly within Israel's history. He does not see Judaism and the church as essentially separate communities, although he never allows the Gentile church full membership in the people of Israel. It is unlikely that Luke's emphasis on continuity with Israel represents an argument to Roman officials for Christianity's legitimation under imperial law (and hence its protection from official persecution). The numerous vignettes in Luke-Acts depicting challenges to the public order from Jesus and his followers (Lk. 13:31ff.; 19:45f.; 22:25–30; Acts 5:27–32; 17:6–9; 19:23–41; 22:21ff.) make such a view quite implausible. Instead, Luke is probably addressing the church at large—by this time predominantly Gentile—so as to strengthen its identity through the message that it is no novelty but the logical outcome of God's ancient dealings with Israel. By highlighting the church's Jewish-Christian heroes and heroines in Acts, Luke implicitly exhorts his Gentile readers to honor the Jewish believers in their midst. For him, these Jews are the lifeblood of the church, its material and spiritual link with empirical Israel. By the time Luke writes in the 80s, Jewish presence is diminishing in the young catholic church, and Jewish believers who practice Torah may already be viewed by the growing Gentile majority as anachronistic. Luke probably finds such a situation quite threatening to the church's well-being. In 6:22f. of the Third Gospel we find a hint that our author knew of or anticipated the official split between church and synagogue. But this plays virtually no role in the panorama of his two-volume work.

Luke divides God's plan for the world's salvation into four major epochs: *(a)* the era of the law and the prophets; *(b)* the days of Jesus; *(c)* the time of the church; and *(d)* the restoration of all things (especially Israel) following Jesus' Parousia. No single epoch entirely supplants its predecessor. Instead, each one embraces and raises to new heights all that has come before. Thus, Jesus does not render the law and the prophets obsolete (Lk. 16:17). Nor does the church replace Israel. Jews within the church represent the beginning of Israel's final renewal, while Gentile believers are seen as an "associate" people of God (Jervell) who share in the eschatological blessings poured out upon empirical Israel. These are, above all, the Spirit and its gifts (Acts 2).

Luke interprets the time of the church as an era of Gentile ascendancy during which Jerusalem will fall into ruin (Lk. 21:24) and the Jewish people will suffer divisions regarding Jesus' identity (Acts 28:23–28). Those Jews who explicitly reject faith in Jesus' Messiahship will find themselves standing outside the renewed Israel of epoch three (Acts 3:19, 22–23). They may even miss out on the messianic banquet at Jesus' Parousia (Lk. 13:23–30; 14:15–24). But their exile from this end-time celebration of salvation will not be permanent (Lk. 13:34–35; 21:24), for they are God's firstborn, his chosen people from the beginning (Lk. 15:25–31). Statements in Luke-Acts about unbelieving Israel's ignorance of God's plan or blindness to it (e.g., Lk. 19:41–42; Acts 3:17; 13:27) must be seen as temporary judgments. This also holds true for Paul's last speech in Acts (28:25–28), which has been wrongly taken by some Christian interpreters as a rejection of the Jews. Throughout Luke-Acts, the fulfillment of Israel's classical hopes (such as the general resurrection, the rebuilding of Jerusalem, the rejuvenation of the land, and the reunion of the twelve tribes) is envisaged. This fulfillment does not apply to the church alone. Luke offers his readers a less imminent form of Parousia expectation than Mark's or Matthew's; nevertheless, he clearly thinks that Jesus will return soon (Lk. 21:29–36).

Of special interest to contemporary Jews and Christians is Luke's attitude toward Pharisees. In the Third Gospel we find much hostility between them and Jesus. But this is juxtaposed with examples of mutual care and respect (Lk. 7:36–50; 13:31). Luke alone tells us that Jesus ate with Pharisees. At table, he acts as a teacher of Pharisees who is genuinely concerned about their eternal welfare (14:12–14). For Luke, the Pharisees play no part in bringing about Jesus' death. Throughout Acts, only one group of them receives criticism: *Christian* Pharisees associated with the Jerusalem church (Acts 15:5ff.). Non-Christian Pharisees are portrayed as a moderate element in Judaism which opposes the persecution of the church (5:33–39; 23:6–9). For Luke, Paul remains a practicing Pharisee during the entire course of his ministry. Taken as a whole, Luke-Acts offers its Gentile readers little incentive for hostility toward the Jewish people or even the Jewish sages at Jamnia in the 80s and 90s.

JOHN

With John's Gospel, the movement toward separation between church and synagogue, already evident in some other New Testament books as a subtheme, reaches a painful and angry climax. The latest stratum of material in the Fourth Gospel presupposes a final departure from Judaism on the part of John's Christian community. In the Evangelist's eyes, this has come about via a decree, probably stemming from the Pharisaic teachers at Jamnia around 85–90 C.E., that Jewish believers will henceforth be regarded as *aposynagōgoi*, "out of the synagogue" (Jn. 9:22; 12:42; 16:2). Earlier stages in the composition of the Fourth Gospel indicate that the Evangelist's congregation held to Jewish worship practices, while at the same time confessing Jesus as the Messiah. In its desire to remain Jewish, this congregation differed from most of the others contemporaneous with it which were either Gentile or mixed and therefore removed from the strict practices of Judaism. It is hard to determine whether the frequent equations of Jesus with God found in John's Gospel came into being after the church-synagogue split, or whether they characterized the Johannine congregation's faith prior to the final schism and so contributed to it. We are on firmer ground in assigning to the post-separation period those passages which *(a)* condemn Jews and Judaism outright or *(b)* see Jesus and Christians as Israel's replacement.

Under *(a)* we may classify the texts that denounce "the Jews" as enemies of Jesus and God (5:16ff.; 6:41, 52; 8:52–59; 10:31ff.; 18:36; 20:19, etc.), along with those which deny to Jews or Judaism any authentic status in God's eyes (5:37–47; 8:39–47; 10:7–8; 15:23–25). The cruelest of these condemnations is a statement by the Johannine Jesus that Jews who oppose him are children not of God or Abraham but of the devil (8:34–47). Under *(b)* we may place texts that portray Jesus as the new temple (2:19ff.) or home of believers (10:9; 14:23), the new Torah (1:17; 7:37–39; 14:6f.), and the true vine (new Israel) into which all who accept his Lordship will come to be engrafted (15:1–7). Behind each of these images is the claim that whenever Jews reject Jesus, they forfeit to Christians their place as God's chosen ones.

The Fourth Gospel presents an extremely difficult challenge to contemporary Jewish-Christian dialogue. If accepted literalistically by Christians, it renders dialogue impossible, for its final redactor clearly believes that Judaism after Jesus has lost all religious value. The ambivalences toward Jews and Judaism which we have detected among the other New Testament writers virtually disappear in this book. "Creative tensions" are resolved into neat and devastating either-or formulas. Now Jesus functions as the one way of access to God *in contrast to Judaism.* The immense Christ of John's community so engulfs the beliefs and practices of his mother religion that he effectively transcends them. Nothing in the Fourth Gospel suggests that this state of affairs will change significantly when the general resurrection occurs.

In fairness, it must be noted that John's community was almost certainly Jewish in origin and would not have thought of itself as apostate. From a history of religions point of view, the Gospel might be classified as a Jewish document in the sense that its guiding images flow from the Hebrew Scriptures and rabbinic thought. But Jews today would surely resist this classification on grounds that John has spoken too strongly against the people of Israel who cannot accept Jesus' Messiahship.

Three Observations

With the possible exception of John, Jesus and the earliest Christian authors whom we have studied show themselves to be quite Jewish. Having reviewed our investigations in order to articulate the nature of each witness's Jewishness, we are now in a position to make some generalizations about the New Testament as a whole.

1. In their respective stances toward Jews and Judaism, Jesus and the authors studied are affected by such variants as:

ethnic consciousness
knowledge of Judaism
actual contacts with Jewish authorities
purpose(s) for writing
convictions about eschatology

involvement in broad, world-historical events and forces and probably many more, including personal eccentricities! The simple fact that all New Testament attitudes are historically conditioned must play a large role in the formation of any contemporary Christian position on Jews and Judaism.

2. One feature common to Jesus and all the New Testament writers whom we have studied is a desire to maintain close connections with the heritage of Israel *as manifested in first-century Judaism.* Such a judgment applies even to the Fourth Gospel, if we take into consideration those passages which reflect an attempt on the part of John's community to continue synagogue worship. This common desire on the part of New Testament Christians to remain inside Judaism was not simply pragmatic, i.e., a tactic to fend off persecution by the Roman government. Above all, it was a passion for unity

with God's chosen people of old. This passion never quite evaporates from the pages of the New Testament, even in John where we must discern reactive feelings of fear, hurt, and anger behind the numerous condemnations of Jews. Many of the ambivalent or paradoxical statements about Judaism made by New Testament writers result from hopes for partnership in Israel which have become complicated by experiences of conflict with the mother religion.

3. Apart from the Fourth Gospel, even "finished" thoughts about Israel in the New Testament remain visibly incomplete (see, above all, Rom. 9–11). The provisional quality of earliest Christian reflection on Jews and Judaism is caused, most directly, by the eschatological world views of Jesus and the New Testament authors. For them, God's mighty acts in first-century Palestine signaled the imminent end of ordinary human history. Jesus and most of his first interpreters looked forward to a literal establishment of God's Kingdom on earth within their own lifetimes.[1] This hope enabled them to hold almost contradictory opinions about Jews and Judaism. On the one hand, they felt, God was doing new things that could not be comprehended within the thought patterns of Judaism (2 Cor. 5:17; Mk. 2:18–22 and parallels). On the other hand, since God always remained faithful to his ancient promises, empirical Israel's preeminence as the chosen people was assumed to continue, even when Gentiles began to experience intimate access to Israel's God through Jesus. In short order, the earliest Christians thought, this same Jesus would descend from heaven to complete God's salvation. According to some New Testament witnesses, Jesus' return would also bring about a harmonious sharing of this salvation by Israel and the church (Rom. 11:25–27; Lk. 13:34–35; 21:20–28). Then all blindness (including the Christian blindness acknowledged in Mt. 25:31–46; 1 Cor. 13:12; 2 Cor. 4:8; Rom. 11:33–34) would be removed, all divisions healed (1 Cor. 15:28). Then everyone would finally receive God's merciful justice (Rom. 11:32). Given the tension of early Christian existence "between the times," it was possible, indeed necessary, to live with unfinished thoughts and unresolved feelings about the relationship between Israel and church. As we might expect, this eschatological tension plays a smaller role in the Fourth Gospel than in other New

Testament books. John believed that God's Final Judgment of the world, which spelled condemnation for "the Jews," was happening already in the ministries of Jesus and his followers (Jn. 3:18f.; 5: 22–29; 12:31, 47f.; 16:7–11). When it came, the end of time would simply ratify what was already visible. For John, Christ's reappearance would bring no surprises.[2]

Levels of Authority in the New Testament

By their examples of word and deed, Jesus and the great majority of the New Testament witnesses mandate us to keep Jewish-Christian relationships alive. They do not do so with equal consistency or clarity. Some authors, especially Paul and Luke, seem "up front" about their hope for Jews who cannot accept Jesus as Messiah. Their struggles to find a place in God's plan for "all Israel" are obvious to any careful reader of their works. Mark does not speculate about Israel's future, but neither does he condemn the Jewish people wholesale for Jesus' death. Although he writes to Gentiles, Mark pictures Jesus as fundamentally loyal to Israel. Still other New Testament writers like John and, to a lesser extent, Matthew feel that their backs are against the wall. Many of their theological formulations are reactions to what they conceive of as injustices committed against them by Jewish authorities. Their positive attitudes toward Jews and Judaism must be discerned more indirectly by getting behind their face statements. To complicate matters further, we find varying degrees of sensitivity to Israel's uniqueness within each individual author. The Paul of Galatians 3 is not identical to the Paul of Romans 9–11.

How shall we respond to this complex situation if we want to take Biblical authority seriously? It is surely illegitimate simply to revel in those passages which appear to promote Jewish-Christian understanding, while ignoring all the others. And yet it seems absolutely necessary to devise some procedure for discerning which parts of the New Testament most clearly reveal God's truth about church and synagogue. As Christians, we begin with the faith-claim that Jesus of Nazareth, crucified and risen, is both Lord and Christ. Thus we naturally incline toward those parts of Scripture which "urge Christ" (Luther's *was Christum treibet*).

This principle is valid as far as it goes. But alongside it we must place those numerous confessions by virtually every New Testament writer that the Lordship and Messiahship of Jesus remain unfinished, still in process.[3] The actual effect of Jesus' exaltation upon the world must appear ambiguous and apprehensible only through faith until it is finally clarified by God at the end of the age (see, e.g., 1 Cor. 15:20–28; Acts 3:19–21). Whereas most New Testament witnesses expected this windup to occur within a short period of time, we have now witnessed two millennia of church history, as well as the sturdy survival of Judaism. If most first-century Jews were blind to Jesus' Messiahship, most first-century Christians were equally blind to God's timetable and hence to the purposes for which he has chosen to "extend" life in this world. One of these purposes would seem to be that we Christians learn humility by acknowledging the liveliness and viability of Judaism. As a consequence of this we should abandon our efforts to convert Jews.

If Paul were alive today, he would have to confess once again: "O the depth of the riches and wisdom and knowledge of God! How unsearchable are his judgments and how inscrutable his ways!" (Rom. 11:33). And then the apostle would probably set about revising the content of that eschatological mystery which he passed on to his Roman readers in the late 50s c.e. (see Rom. 11:25–32). Among other things, we would have to reckon with three historical developments that he never foresaw: the transformation of life in Christ into a separate religion called Christianity, the periodic persecution of Jews by members of this religion, and the Holocaust.[4] No view of New Testament authority that fails to incorporate this limited vision on the part of the earliest believers can be called adequate.

On the positive side, we may affirm that those New Testament writings or parts of writings which encourage and equip us to wrestle with the issues listed above will finally ring most true. In using such sources, we shall discover that they give almost equal weight both to God's ancient promises and to God's disturbing preference for new ways of fulfilling them. New Testament writers and passages that do not fall into this category can often be explained in the light of sociological and/or psychological pressures which have combined to produce constricted thinking. A prime example would be Matthew's heightened polemic against the Pharisees which he himself develops and reads back into Jesus' ministry as a result of his own post-70 conflicts with Jamnia rabbis. On the other hand, as we have seen, this same Matthew retains a solid residue of goodwill toward the traditions, institutions, practices, and people of Israel. It is this, not his all too obvious polemic, which we Christians must learn to see as foundational to his faith in Jesus. As we noted at the end of Chapter 6, we have no warrant for altering a particular New Testament text or excising it from our canon. What we need to change is our perception of the text, for only by reading a passage or book in its fullest possible historical milieu can we come to a proper appreciation of the author's intentions. Only by this means can we develop adequate criteria for levels of authority within the New Testament as a whole and within each of its individual authors.

Using the New Testament in Dialogue

Before we Christians venture forth into conversations with our Jewish neighbors on matters of mutual concern, we need to learn precisely what our New Testament Scriptures have to say about Jewish-Christian relationships. This axiom has served as my guiding principle in the construction of the present book. But how do we prepare ourselves for dialogue? Then, having done our homework, how do we employ our knowledge most fruitfully in ecumenical conversations?

Dr. Samuel Sandmel suggests that the dual task confronting Christians today is first, to identify anti-Semitism within the New Testament, and second, to transcend it.[5] Although I prefer the term "anti-Judaism" (see Foreword), I agree with Dr. Sandmel's statement of the agenda. I simply want to supplement it with the observation, which I have attempted to document in the pages above, that both the identifying of attitudes hostile to Jews or Judaism and the transcending of those attitudes are *best accomplished with resources provided by the New Testament.* With the possible exception of John, New Testament writers are not fundamentally anti-Judaistic. On the contrary, when we read them in their historical contexts, we are usually led by them toward a greater appreciation of Israel's heritage and our Gentile indebtedness to it.

Far from renouncing our New Testament Scriptures or shying away from them in embarrassment, we Christians can honor them as an inspired record of struggles to interpret both old and new acts of God, without shortchanging either. Of course ambivalence, misunderstanding, and anger often color these struggles, but their authenticity is not thereby negated. From the very beginning, relationships between Israel and the movement springing from Jesus were destined to be both problematic and promising. My belief is that today, with the help of historical-critical scholarship and a new Christian openness toward Judaism after the Holocaust, we can read the New Testament in such a way as to recover what was and still is most promising.

Let us now move on to specifics, first with regard to our preparation for dialogue.

1. When interpreting the New Testament for any purpose, we must begin by reading it carefully. There is no substitute for accurate knowledge of content. We may employ various guides to sharpen our perceptions, but in the end we must do our own conversing with the ancient authors.

2. In addition to our Bible reading, we shall want to engage representative voices from the new wealth of contemporary scholarship by Jews and Christians which focuses on the history of first-century Palestine.[6] Judaism at the time of Jesus was far more diverse than most Christians suspect, and this complexity plays an important role in the production of the New Testament.

3. Since education takes place on many levels, we must learn to deal sensitively with Jewish-Christian relationships at diverse

moments in the life of the church. These include those frequent occasions when questions about Jewish tradition or practice enter our Christian consciousness but no Jews are present.

a. Scriptural readings in public worship which might arouse or feed hostility against Jews may be prefaced with explanations about their origins and/or supplemented with more positive texts by the same author.

b. Liturgical forms which imply that "the Jews" are responsible for Jesus' death require careful revision.[7] So do those which treat the church as "new Israel" or "true Israel." On the other hand, it is possible to build upon some liturgical expressions already in use which properly distinguish between Israel and church.[8] These could be highlighted in educational sessions or narrated services so that as people employ them Sunday after Sunday a positive reinforcement can take place. In addition, supportive prayers for neighboring Jewish congregations, especially during the celebration of their holy days, might become a regular part of our Sunday worship. Denominational and parish calendars could encourage this practice by including the dates of Jewish festivals.

c. Church school teachers, especially those charged with the training of youngsters and teen-agers, can be helped in their role as Biblical interpreters to accentuate the positive attitudes toward Jews and Judaism held by New Testament writers.[9] This requires the development of a fairly sophisticated approach to the Bible among teachers, but the times call us to such expertise.

When we have achieved a reasonable degree of confidence in our knowledge of what the New Testament sources actually say about Jewish-Christian relationships, we can begin to make efforts toward building or strengthening long-term interaction with the Jewish groups known to us. Much of this can be done on a local congregational level or under the auspices of regional ministerial associations.[10] One important point to remember is that dialogue with Jews will seldom center on the New Testament as such. Nor should it, at least in the beginning.[11] The New Testament nurtures our Christian faith and, along with the Hebrew Scriptures, helps us bring this faith to fruition in love. It stimulates us to honor God's ancient people and seek out community with them. But it does not furnish us with a detailed set of guidelines for contemporary discussions with Jews. The New Testament's very incompleteness with regard to Jews and Judaism encourages us to anticipate the Spirit's guidance. For it may well be God's Spirit who is fashioning this new era of widespread mutual respect among Jews and Christians, an opportunity unprecedented in the church's history.

When dialogues do take place, they will form around a great variety of issues, such as: social-political problems faced by Jew and Christian alike (e.g., intermarriage, ecumenical social action projects, or relations with local and national governments); efforts to combat anti-Semitism; attitudes toward the state of Israel; and particular aspects of faith or practice, the discussion of which will benefit both partners. Some of these discussions will prove emotionally trying, for we must work to overcome centuries of mistrust.[12] From the Christian side, sustaining power in hard times can emerge from the good news announced by the New Testament that despite substantial differences, Jews and Christians really do share a common origin and a common destiny. How can we mend our family relationships along the way?

Israel Without and Within

The Christian church does not supersede the Jewish people as God's elect nation. We Gentile Christians are an associate people of God (Luke-Acts). We are "honorary Jews"[13] who praise God alongside Israel (Rom. 15:7–10). Our life in Christ always means life in company with Israel. Of this we are constantly reminded by the New Testament writers, who demonstrate a rootedness in Judaism, an intimacy with it which is absolutely fundamental to their Christian identities.

How can we think most fruitfully today about our complex relationship with Jews and Judaism? A story from the Hebrew Scriptures may help us to discern an image for dialogue in our time:

> [Jacob] arose and took his two wives, his two maids, and his eleven children, and crossed the ford of the Jabbok. He took them and sent them across the stream, and likewise everything that he had. And Jacob was left alone; and a man wrestled with him until the breaking of the day. When the man saw that he did not prevail against Jacob, he touched the hollow of his thigh; and Jacob's thigh was put out of joint as he wrestled with him. Then he said, "Let me go, for the day is breaking." But Jacob said, "I will not let you go, unless you bless me." And he said to him, "What is your name?" And he said, "Jacob." Then he said, "Your name shall no more be called Jacob, but Israel, for you have striven with God and with men, and have prevailed." Then Jacob asked him, "Tell me, I pray, your name." But he said, "Why is it that you ask my name?" And there he blessed him. So Jacob called the name of the place Peniel, saying, "For I have seen God face to face, and yet my life is preserved." (Gen. 32: 22–30)

This story is suggestive at many levels, but it will probably be most helpful to focus especially on Jacob's struggle and name change. In wrestling with God's messenger (or God himself!), Jacob becomes Israel. He both receives an extraordinary blessing and, like his grandfather Abraham, takes on the bearing of God's wider blessing to all nations (see Gen. 12:1–3). Along with other peoples of the world, we Christians stand to inherit handsomely from Jacob's struggle. But we also share that struggle here and now in quite a special way. To us followers of Jesus, the witness of Jacob's descendants throughout history brings a particular revelation from God, without which we cannot gain our own true identities. The ongoing struggle of the Jewish people for survival and authentic life ("Israel" probably means "he who strives with God") is a constant source of blessing for us, *if* we acknowledge our unique kinship with them and honor them as elder brothers and sisters. Empirical Israel, embodied in the Jews and Judaism of our day, is a concrete sign of God's presence with us.

But there is more. We Christians confess that through Jesus we have come to know the Spirit of God in our hearts (Gal. 4:6; 2 Cor.

3:3; Rom. 8:9–15). That is a bold claim which carries great responsibility along with it (Ezek. 36:27). The Spirit within not only witnesses to our chosenness by God but also sensitizes us to Israel's unique place in God's plan of salvation (see Rom. 9:1–5). If we Christians are a charismatic people (1 Cor. 12:1–7), Israel has been one much longer.[14] The God who bestows his Spirit on us is none other than the God of Abraham, Isaac, and Jacob; and he does not forsake their descendants by creating the church. In blessing us Gentiles through Jesus, God means always to bless his ancient people as well (Rom. 11:25–27). Though we Gentile Christians are not, strictly speaking, members of Israel, we nevertheless carry a living and passionate link with Israel in our hearts. If we ally ourselves with the struggles of contemporary Jews (Israel without) and attend to the voice of God's Spirit (Israel within), Jewish-Christian dialogue will bear wondrous fruit. The New Testament stands ready to serve us in the broadening and deepening of that dialogue.

NOTES

Foreword

1. I have verified this information with Rabbi Solomon S. Bernards, Director of the Anti-Defamation League's Department of Interreligious Cooperation.

2. See "Let's Clear Up the Fuzziness and Still Be Friends," *Christianity Today*, Vol. 21, No. 12 (March 18, 1977), pp. 29f. The editorial writer takes particular umbrage at the views of British clergyman James W. Parkes, who is quoted as saying: "The modern scholar has no difficulty in distinguishing between the preaching of Jesus and the contemporary picture of the teaching of the scribes and Pharisees in the Gospel of Mark, from the sweeping and preposterous generalizations attributed to Jesus in the infamous chapter 23 of the Gospel of Matthew, or the still more absurd statement in the Fourth Gospel that, almost before Jesus had opened his mouth, 'the Jews' sought to kill him (John 5:16–18)." I myself do not agree with the way Parkes has stated his case; his rhetoric shows that he has made too little effort to understand the origins of these Gospel texts. Nevertheless, as our exegetical chapters will demonstrate, Parkes's reading of the evidence is not entirely off base.

3. *Christianity Today*, Vol. 21, No. 15 (May 6, 1977), p. 8. All elisions have been made by the editors of the magazine.

4. Rosemary Ruether, *Faith and Fratricide: The Theological Roots of Anti-Semitism* (Seabury Press, 1974). See especially Ch. 2, "The Growing Estrangement: The Rejection of the Jews in the New Testament." T. A. Indinopulos and R. B. Ward have challenged one aspect of Ruether's position by arguing that "the appearance of anti-Judaic thought in certain documents in the New Testament does not lead to the conclusion that anti-Judaism is necessarily the left hand of christology." See "Is Christology

Inherently Anti-Semitic?" *Journal of the American Academy of Religion,* Vol. 45, No. 2 (June 1977), pp. 196ff.

5. Among Samuel Sandmel's books on Jewish-Christian dialogue are the following:

> *We Jews and Jesus.* Oxford University Press, 1965.
> *We Jews and You Christians.* J. B. Lippincott Co., 1967.
> *The First Christian Century in Judaism and Christianity: Certainties and Uncertainties.* Oxford University Press, 1969.
> *The Genius of Paul: A Study in History.* Schocken Books, 1970.
> *Judaism and Christian Beginnings.* Oxford University Press, 1978.

6. Samuel Sandmel, *Anti-Semitism in the New Testament?* (Fortress Press, 1978), esp. pp. 154–165.

7. Paul and Matthew were certainly of Jewish parentage; so, I believe, were most members of the community that produced the Fourth Gospel (Chapter 6). The Jewish origins of Mark and Luke may be questioned. But Mark, a Semite of some kind, presents an essentially Jewish picture of Jesus (Chapter 3), and Luke was probably a friend of Judaism or even a proselyte before he became a Christian (Chapter 5, n. 22). Among the New Testament books that are not extensively treated below, I take the following to have been authored by Jews: James, Ephesians, I Peter, the Johannine letters, Jude, and Revelation.

8. The RSV translation of 2 Cor. 5:17 ("If any one is in Christ, he is a new creation") does not do justice to the epistemological and cosmological dimensions of this passage. When rendered literally, the Greek sentence in question comes out: "If any one in Christ, new creation." We must supply the verbs, and the context in 2 Cor. 5 weighs against concluding that Paul wishes to equate the person in Christ with the new creation. A preferable translation would be: "If any one is in Christ, he or she perceives a new creation." See James Louis Martyn, "Epistemology at the Turn of the Ages: 2 Corinthians 5:16" in *Christian History and Interpretation: Studies Presented to John Knox,* ed. by W. R. Farmer, C. F. D. Moule, and R. R. Niebuhr (Cambridge University Press, 1967), pp. 269–287.

9. Similarly, the word "Israelite" in the New Testament always means simply "Jew," without regard to whether the person described believes in Jesus' Messiahship or not. See Jn. 1:47; Acts 2:22; 3:12; 5:35; 13:16; 21:28; Rom. 9:4; 11:1; 2 Cor. 11:22.

10. It must be admitted, however, that the later levels of the Fourth Gospel picture Jesus and Christian believers as transcending not only the Judaism of their day (Jn. 8:39–47; 15:1–11) but also the experience of ancient Israel (1:17; 6:31–33; 10:7–8).

Chapter 1
JESUS AND THE FIRST CHURCH: AT HOME IN JUDAISM

1. John A. T. Robinson has recently argued that all four Gospels came into being much earlier, between 50 and 60. See his *Redating the New Testament* (Westminster Press, 1976), pp. 13–30, 86–117, 254–311. Scholarly reaction to this redating has been understandably slow since the revisions that Robinson proposes are major ones. One important review, however, concludes that Robinson has not established his major thesis. See R. M. Grant, *Journal of Biblical Literature,* Vol. 97 (June 1978), pp. 294–296. In my view, the strongest evidence for a post-70 dating of Matthew is the assumption evident throughout his Gospel that the Pharisees control Judaism. But this one-party leadership did not emerge until after the Jewish-Roman war of 66–70. As for Luke, his Gospel presupposes an extended period of time after the destruction of Jerusalem—probably the time during which he writes—when "Jerusalem will be trodden down by Gentiles." The Holy City is to regain its glory (presumably at Jesus' return from heaven) when "the times of the Gentiles are fulfilled." (Lk. 21:20–24; unique to the Third Gospel). For further evidence leading to a post-70 dating of Matthew and Luke, see Chapters 4 and 5.

2. All three Evangelists locate this story between Jesus' blessing of the children and his third passion prediction. Matthew, however, inserts the parable of the laborers in the vineyard just before the passion prediction (see Mt. 19–20).

3. Géza Vermès, *Jesus the Jew* (Macmillan Publishing Co., 1973), pp. 43–57.

4. *Ibid.,* p. 54.

5. David Flusser, "The Son of Man: Jesus in the Context of History," *The Crucible of Christianity,* ed. by Arnold Toynbee (World Publishing Co., 1969), p. 225.

6. Cited from mTaan 3:8, by Vermès, in *Jesus the Jew,* p. 70.

7. Vermès, *Jesus the Jew,* pp. 69–72.

8. *Ibid.,* pp. 74–75.

9. Flusser, in Toynbee, *The Crucible of Christianity,* p. 225.

10. In three New Testament books, "false witnesses" allude to a saying of Jesus that he himself would destroy the Temple (Mk. 14:57–58; Mt. 26:61; Acts 6:13–14). In Matthew and Mark, reference is also made to a claim on his part that he would build a new temple. The fourth Evangelist records a similar saying of Jesus just after narrating the cleansing of the

Temple: "Destroy this temple, and in three days I will raise it up" (Jn. 2:19). According to John, "he spoke of the temple of his body" (2:21). The origin of this confused tradition must remain speculative, but it is just possible that Jesus *did* connect himself, as Messiah, with the Jerusalem Temple's destruction. Even so, that would represent no condemnation of Judaism or the Temple per se, but rather a conviction that a perfect, eschatological temple must replace the imperfect one built by Herod. Such ideas were held elsewhere in first-century Judaism. See, e.g., the recently published Temple Scroll from Qumran.

11. See R. H. Hiers, "Purification of the Temple: Preparation for the Kingdom of God," *Journal of Biblical Literature,* Vol. 90 (March 1971), pp. 82–90.

12. Bammel, Ernst, ed. *The Trial of Jesus: Cambridge Studies in Honour of C. F. D. Moule.* London: SCM Press, 1970. Protestant and Roman Catholic.

Sloyan, Gerard S. *Jesus on Trial: The Development of the Passion Narratives and Their Historical and Ecumenical Implications,* ed. with an introduction by John Reumann. Fortress Press, 1973. Roman Catholic and Protestant.

Wilson, William Riley. *The Execution of Jesus: A Judicial, Literary, and Historical Investigation.* Charles Scribner's Sons, 1970. Protestant.

Winter, Paul. *On the Trial of Jesus.* Berlin: Töpelmann Verlag, 1961. Jewish.

13. Mark and Matthew report that *some* Pharisees plotted against Jesus (Mk. 12:13; Mt. 22:15) and early in his ministry even planned to bring about his destruction (Mk. 3:6; Mt. 12:14). But these Pharisees, whoever they were, are never linked by the Evangelists with the trial.

Chapter 2
PAUL: ON THE WAY TO UNITY

1. See Joseph Klausner, *From Jesus to Paul,* tr. by William F. Stinespring (Beacon Press, 1961); Martin Buber, *Two Types of Faith,* tr. by Norman P. Goldhawk (Harper & Brothers, 1951, 1961); F. C. Baur, *The Church History of the First Three Centuries,* tr. and ed. by A. Menzies (London, 1878), I, pp. 44–66, 75–77; Adolf von Harnack, "The Founder of Christian Civilization," in *What Is Christianity?* tr. by T. B. Saunders (New York, 1901).

2. Rudolf Bultmann, "The Kerygma of the Hellenistic Church Aside from Paul," in *Theology of the New Testament,* Vol. I, tr. by Kendrick Grobel (Charles Scribner's Sons, 1951); Archibald M. Hunter, *Paul and His Predecessors* (Westminster Press, 1961); Wayne A. Meeks, "The Christian Proteus," in *The Writings of St. Paul,* ed. by Wayne A. Meeks (W. W. Norton & Co., 1972), p. 440.

3. See, e.g., William David Davies, *Paul and Rabbinic Judaism* (London: S.P.C.K., 1962), and Ed Parish Sanders, *Paul and Palestinian Judaism* (Fortress Press, 1977).

4. B. Pearson, "1 Thessalonians 2:13–16: A Deutero-Pauline Interpolation," *Harvard Theological Review,* Vol. 64 (1971), pp. 79–94.

5. Another possibility is that the phrase "at last" *(eis telos)* in 1 Thess. 2:16 should be translated "until the end," that is, "temporarily." See Johannes Munck, *Christ and Israel,* tr. by Ingeborg Nixon (Fortress Press, 1967), p. 64.

6. Krister Stendahl, "The Apostle Paul and the Introspective Conscience of the West" in *Paul Among Jews and Gentiles* (Fortress Press, 1976), p. 85; see also pp. 3ff. Stendahl has recently defended this view against objections by E. P. Sanders in "A Response," *Union Seminary Quarterly Review,* Vol. 33 (Spring and Summer 1978), p. 190.

7. Some have pointed to Gal. 6:15f. as the one exception: "For neither circumcision counts for anything, nor uncircumcision, but a new creation. Peace and mercy be upon all who walk by this rule, upon the Israel of God." But this translation must be challenged. Literally, the last sentence reads: "And as many as walk by this rule, peace upon them and mercy also *(kai)* upon the Israel of God." It is probable that here, as in Romans, Paul distinguishes between those who live by the standards of the new creation (believers) and those who claim status as God's people by virtue of their ancient election (Israel). In Phil. 3:3, Paul refers to Christians as "the circumcision" (the adjective "true," interjected by RSV translators, does not appear in the Greek text). Here the apostle is not claiming that the church has replaced the Jewish nation as God's elect people; instead, he is polemicizing against *Christians* who insist that physical circumcision is necessary for salvation. See H. Koester, "The Purpose of a Pauline Fragment (Phil. 3)," *New Testament Studies,* Vol. 8 (1961/62), pp. 317–322.

Chapter 3
MARK: A JEWISH GOSPEL FOR GENTILES

1. Cited by Michael Grant, *The Jews in the Roman World* (Charles Scribner's Sons, 1973), p. 202. Grant notes that Josephus' figures may be somewhat inflated but that the real losses were nevertheless "appallingly high."

2. William David Davies, *The Setting of the Sermon on the Mount* (Cambridge University Press, 1964), pp. 256f.

3. The exact dates remain obscure, and it is not certain that the two apostles died at the same time. Paul may have been executed prior to the Neronic persecution of 64 since he was already under arrest by Roman authorities for some years before that time (see Acts 21–28).

4. Grant, *The Jews in the Roman World*, pp. 61–64, 205.

5. *Ibid.*, pp. 181f., 205, 212.

6. The Semitic words *not* translated are usually liturgical expressions such as *amen, hosanna,* or *abba,* which would have been understood by Gentile Christians in Mark's day. See, e.g., the Aramaic petition *Maranatha* in 1 Cor. 16:22.

7. Yet Mark himself seems not very well acquainted with the nuances of Palestinian Judaism in Jesus' day. See D. E. Nineham, *Saint Mark* (Westminster Press, 1978), pp. 193f. on Mk. 7:3–4; and Sloyan, *Jesus on Trial*, p. 61 on Mk. 14:63f. Perhaps Mark was a Diaspora Jew who had learned Hebrew or Aramaic but who had never visited the Holy Land. Alternatively, he may have been a Semitic Gentile, e.g., a Syrian, who lived close enough to Palestine to acquire some knowledge of Jewish practices there but was misinformed on certain matters.

8. As we noted above, many, or perhaps most, of the Christians living in and around Jerusalem fled to Pella before the war broke out in 66. But on grounds of historical probability we must suppose that some believers remained behind, especially in the Judean countryside.

9. The fact that Mark can refer to Christians as "the elect" does not alter this judgment. In Mk. 13:20, 27, the chosen ones envisioned are those to whom faith has been granted (see 4:10–12); but no claim is made that these people have *replaced* Israel as God's special people. Election is expanded, but without repudiating the ancient promises.

10. Grant, *The Jews in the Roman World*, p. 215.

11. Ruether, *Faith and Fratricide*, p. 92.

12. Grant, *The Jews in the Roman World*, p. 318, n. 38.

13. The word "scribe" seems to be a nonparty term. Some scribes associated with the Pharisees, while others linked themselves with the high priests. See, e.g., Mk. 15:1. The two sets of scribes could be expected to take quite different positions on Jesus' ministry. Matthew 13:52 suggests that even Christians had their scribes.

14. See Sloyan, *Jesus on Trial,* pp. 63, 69, 71f., 128–130, and Sandmel, *Anti-Semitism in the New Testament?* pp. 136f.

15. Traditions about feasts and fasts differed considerably from group to group in first-century Judaism and always became a point for lively debate.

16. Vincent Taylor, *The Gospel According to Mark* (Macmillan Co., 1959), p. 596, and Nineham, *Saint Mark,* p. 430.

17. Donald Juel has made a strong case for connecting the tearing of the Temple veil with Mk. 14:58, where false witnesses at Jesus' trial charge him with stating: "I will destroy this temple that is made with hands, and in three days I will build another, not made with hands." According to Juel, Mark understands this charge to be false on the literal level: Jesus never made any such statement. On the other hand, Mark's readers are also to see that at a deeper level the unfounded accusation turns out to be true. The origin of the believing community three days after Jesus' crucifixion spells the beginning of the temple not made with hands. See *Messiah and Temple: The Trial of Jesus in the Gospel of Mark* (Scholars Press, 1977), pp. 204–215. Obviously, both the destruction and the building referred to in Mk. 14:58 take place only prefiguratively in the Gospel. It is unlikely that Mark conceives of an earthly process whereby the church in his own day will replace the Jerusalem Temple. For him, replacement on the historical level is not the issue. The chief function of the prophecy attributed to Jesus in 14:58 is to contrast the worldly, temporal nature of the present Temple with the heavenly, eternal quality of the Christian community. According to Mark, Jesus himself "destroys" the Temple only in the sense that his death puts a symbolic end to its exclusivism. The risen Christ plays no role in Marcan prophecies concerning the Temple's final destruction (13:1ff.). Indeed, our Evangelist continues to think of the historical Temple as a holy place whose desecration will be abominable (13:14). Mark's point in 14:58 is that after Jesus' resurrection the Temple is no longer God's only dwelling place; nor is it the most lasting one.

18. Ruether, *Faith and Fratricide,* p. 87.

19. To chapter 13 of his book, *The Jews in the Roman World,* Michael Grant applies the title "Jewish Survival: The Menace of the Gospels." In so doing, he adds unnecessary fuel to a tragic fire.

Chapter 4
MATTHEW: A CLAIM ON ISRAEL'S LEADERSHIP

1. Werner G. Kümmel, *Introduction to the New Testament,* rev. ed., tr. by Howard Clark Kee (Abingdon Press, 1975), pp. 107, 112–115.

2. *Ibid.,* pp. 110–112.

3. C. H. Kraeling, "The Jewish Community at Antioch," *Journal of Biblical Literature,* Vol. 51 (1932), pp. 153–154.

4. See, e.g., R. Travers Herford, tr., *Pirke Aboth: The Ethics of the Talmud. Sayings of the Fathers* (Schocken Books, 1962), p. 119; Davies, *The Setting of the Sermon on the Mount,* p. 276; James Louis Martyn, *History and Theology in the Fourth Gospel* (Harper & Row, Publishers, 1968), p. 36.

5. If so, Matthew's purpose would be to show how the words of Jesus in Mt. 23:1–3, well known among Jewish Christians, must now be reinterpreted in the light of harsher sayings by the Messiah.

6. Krister Stendahl describes Matthew's Gospel as a textbook for teachers and church leaders based on principles of Biblical interpretation found in the synagogues. See *The School of St. Matthew and Its Use of the Old Testament* (Uppsala: Almqvist & Wiksell, 1954), pp. 31–35 and *passim,* esp. pp. 216–217.

7. Matthew must have thought of himself as such a scribe. See L. Cope, *Matthew: A Scribe Trained for the Kingdom of Heaven* (The Catholic Biblical Association, 1976). Cope presents convincing evidence that Mt. 13:52 is a self-designation.

8. Davies, *The Setting of the Sermon on the Mount,* pp. 415–433.

9. Gerd Theissen, "Itinerant Radicalism: The Tradition of Jesus Sayings from the Perspective of the Sociology of Literature," tr. by A. Wire, *Radical Religion,* Vol. 2 (1975), p. 89. See also Theissen's *Sociology of Early Palestinian Christianity,* tr. by John Bowden (Fortress Press, 1978), pp. 11, 51.

10. Johannes Hoekendijk quotes from a letter by the Jewish philosopher-educator Franz Rosenzweig to his friend Rosenstock: "You Christians are all right in stating that 'nobody comes to the Father, except through Jesus.' Tell the story. We are already with the Father." See Eva Fleischner (ed.), *Auschwitz: Beginning of a New Era? Reflections on the Holocaust* (KTAV Publishing House, 1977), p. 134.

11. Michael Grant *(The Jews in the Roman World,* p. 217) and Ruether *(Faith and Fratricide,* p. 72) seem to have missed this point since they wrongly attribute to Matthew the teaching that only those who believe in Jesus as Messiah can consider themselves part of Israel.

12. Norman Perrin, *Rediscovering the Teaching of Jesus* (Harper & Row Publishers, 1967), p. 161.

13. There is no indication in Matthew's Gospel, however, that the Evangelist insists upon physical circumcision for male Gentiles. He may think of Gentile converts as "God-fearers," that is, people who obey all the Torah laws but circumcision.

Chapter 5
LUKE-ACTS: ROOTS IN ISRAEL'S HISTORY

1. The Greek word which I have translated "instructed" is *katēchēthēs.* It is a form of the verb *katēcheō,* from which our English "catechesis" derives. By Luke's time, *katēchēsis* had acquired the technical meaning of "instruction in Christian teachings" (see 1 Cor. 14:19; Gal. 6:6; Acts 18:25). For further evidence that Luke writes especially to edify *Christians,* consult Ernst Käsemann, "Ephesians and Acts" in Leander Keck and James Louis Martyn (eds.), *Studies in Luke-Acts* (Abingdon Press, 1966), pp. 288–297; Jacob Jervell, *Luke and the People of God* (Augsburg Publishing House, 1972), pp. 13–39; and Paul Minear, "Dear Theo. The Kerygmatic Intention and Claim of the Book of Acts," *Interpretation* (April 1973), pp. 133–137, 146.

2. Hans Conzelmann was the first to highlight Luke's interest in the stages of salvation history and to explore these as a fundamental feature of his theology. See *The Theology of St. Luke,* tr. by Geoffrey Buswell (Harper & Brothers, 1960).

3. The phrase is Jervell's. See *Luke and the People of God,* pp. 41–74.

4. Of the Gentile believers who are specifically *named* by Luke in Acts only one, the proconsul of Cyprus, Sergius Paulus, is not singled out as a God-fearer or proselyte to Judaism; but even he shows Jewish sympathies, for one of his advisers is the Jewish prophet Bar-Jesus (see Acts 13:4–12). Luke does not tell us whether the believers Erastus (19:22), Sopater, Aristarchus, Secundus, Gaius, Trophimus (20:4), and Eutychus (20:7–12) were Jews or Gentiles. Their Greco-Roman names tell us nothing about their national origins and religious affiliations, since many first-century Jews bore such names.

5. Ernst Haenchen, *The Acts of the Apostles, A Commentary,* tr. by Bernard Noble and Gerald Shinn (Westminster Press, 1971), pp. 72–75; Reginald H. Fuller, *A Critical Introduction to the New Testament* (London: Gerald Duckworth & Co., 1966), p. 120.

6. See, e.g., Is. 61; Test. Levi 18:9; and Jervell, *Luke and the People of God*, pp. 41–43, 65–69.

7. Schuyler Brown, *Apostasy and Perseverance in the Theology of Luke* (Rome: Pontifical Biblical Institute, 1969), p. 64.

8. Cited by Haenchen, in *The Acts of the Apostles*, p. 451, n. 1.

9. Jervell, *Luke and the People of God*, pp. 143–147.

10. Arthur W. Wainwright, "Luke and the Restoration of the Kingdom to Israel," *The Expository Times*, Vol. 89 (Dec. 1977), pp. 76–79. See also Eric Franklin, *Christ the Lord: A Study in the Purpose and Theology of Luke-Acts* (Westminster Press, 1975), p. 130.

11. Wainwright, "Luke and the Restoration of the Kingdom to Israel," pp. 76–79.

12. Luke distinguishes God's Kingdom from that of Jesus. The latter, Jesus' rule in Israel through the church, can be thought of in terms of a great meal ("at my table in my kingdom," Lk. 22:30). See also Acts 2:29–47 and note 7, above.

13. Luke's account of the rich man and Lazarus in Lk. 16:19–31 tells us nothing about the *ultimate* fate of the former, since Hades could be understood as a temporary location where souls reside prior to the Final Judgment (see Lk. 14:14). Moreover, the rich man's descent into Hades occurs because he has not shared his wealth more equitably with his fellow Jew Lazarus, not because he has failed to recognize Jesus as Messiah.

14. Franklin, *Christ the Lord*, pp. 114f.

15. Rosemary Ruether counts about 45 occurrences of the term "the Jews" as a hostile symbol in Acts. See *Faith and Fratricide*, pp. 89f. Using the Moulton-Geden *Concordance to the Greek New Testament* and restricting my search to *hoi Ioudaioi*, I find 30 negative meanings, 10 positive ones, and 13 neutral ones. Of the 30 negative references (in all of them Jews are depicted as hostile toward Christians), at least 18 refer to particular groups of Jews. Not one of the 30 could be understood as applicable to all Jews at all times. These data call into question Ruether's inference that Luke sees "the Jews" chiefly and uniformly as opponents.

16. In Luke, lawyers and scribes receive harsher judgment from Jesus than do the Pharisees (compare Lk. 11:39–44 with 11:45–52; 20:45–47 and contrast these sections with Mt. 23).

17. Jervell, *Luke and the People of God*, pp. 185–199.

18. Luke 4:31, which makes a point of informing readers that Capernaum is a city in Galilee (contrast Mk. 1:21), suggests that Luke thought he was

directing his Gospel to people who knew little about the geography of Palestine—most likely Gentiles.

19. Feelings against Jews ran high in the Empire as a whole during the decades following the 66–70 war (see above, p.65). Even if Gentile Christians did not share fully in this hostility, they would probably be moving toward the conclusion that they, not Jewish Christians, were the wave of the future in Christ's Kingdom. For them, Jewish Christians must have appeared increasingly odd and marginal.

20. So Käsemann, in Keck and Martyn, *Studies in Luke-Acts,* pp. 296f.

21. Here Luke has much in common with the Jewish-Christian author of Ephesians who addresses his Gentile readers as an elder brother: "Therefore remember that at one time you Gentiles in the flesh, called the uncircumcision by what is called the circumcision, which is made in the flesh by hands—remember that you were at that time separated from Christ, alienated from the commonwealth of Israel, and strangers to the covenants of promise, having no hope and without God in the world. But now in Christ Jesus you who once were far off have been brought near in the blood of Christ. For he is our peace, who has made us both one, and has broken down the dividing wall of hostility, by abolishing in his flesh the law of commandments and ordinances, that he might create in himself one new man in place of the two, so making peace, and might reconcile us both to God in one body through the cross, thereby bringing the hostility to an end. And he came and preached peace to you who were far off and peace to those who were near; for through him we both have access in one Spirit to the Father. So then you are no longer strangers and sojourners, but you are fellow citizens with the saints and members of the household of God" (Eph. 2:11–19). On one level, this text affirms the equality before God of Gentile believers with Jewish believers. Nevertheless, a certain primacy of honor remains with those who have always been "saints and members of the household of God," namely, Israel. For further similarities between Ephesians and Acts, see Käsemann, in Keck and Martyn, *Studies in Luke-Acts,* pp. 288–297.

22. Luke's intimate knowledge of the LXX, his emphasis on the church's continuity with Judaism, and his obvious sympathy for Jewish or Jewish-tending Christians make it at least plausible that he himself was a Hellenistic Jew or a proselyte to Judaism prior to his conversion.

Chapter 6
JOHN: A PAINFUL BREAK WITH JUDAISM

1. For a description of the process leading to this synagogue ban, see Martyn, *History and Theology in the Fourth Gospel,* pp. 3–41.

2. Raymond E. Brown, *The Gospel According to John,* I–XII, The Anchor Bible (Doubleday & Co., 1966), pp. xxxiv ff.

3. In Jn. 5:2ff. and 19:13 we find references to places in Jerusalem which are not mentioned by the Synoptic writers but have now been verified archaeologically. An eyewitness account of Jesus' death, likewise absent from the Synoptic accounts, seems to be preserved in 19:31–35.

4. A British scholar, Aileen Guilding, has attempted to show that in the Fourth Gospel, Jesus' teachings at the festivals are represented as sermons on the lectionary readings associated with those festivals in the synagogue calendar. Guilding's arguments seem strongest for Jn. 6, where Jesus' words center upon Ex. 16 and allude to Num. 11 and Gen. 3. The Old Testament chapters mentioned occur in an ancient three-year cycle of synagogue readings prescribed for Passover. See *The Fourth Gospel and Jewish Worship* (Oxford University Press, 1966) and Raymond E. Brown, *The Gospel According to John* pp. 278f. It must be noted, however, that scholars disagree about whether such a uniform lectionary existed as early as the first century C.E.

5. The phrase is Martyn's. Our discussion is indebted to his thorough exposition of the Evangelist's once-upon-a-time/now thinking. See *History and Theology in the Fourth Gospel,* especially pp. 40f. and 135–142.

6. *Ibid.,* pp. 10ff.

7. In the Synoptic Gospels, Jesus also predicts death for believers (Mt. 24:21; Mk. 13:12; Lk. 21:16), but the executions referred to in these texts seem to be at the hands of "all nations" (Mt. 24:9), not the Jews.

8. See Martyn, *History and Theology in the Fourth Gospel,* pp. 40ff.

9. A type of "replacement" thinking occurs in the letter to the Hebrews. There we encounter such relections as the following: "[Jewish priests] serve a copy and shadow of the heavenly sanctuary. . . . But as it is, Christ has obtained a ministry which is as much more excellent than the old as the covenant which he mediates is better, since it is enacted on better promises. For if the first covenant had been faultless, there would have been no occasion for a second. . . . In speaking of a new covenant [the Holy Spirit through the prophet Jeremiah] treats the first

as obsolete. And what is becoming obsolete and growing old is ready to vanish away" (Heb. 8:5–7, 13). "For since the law has but a shadow of the good things to come instead of the true form of these realities, it can never, by the same sacrifices which are continually offered year by year, make perfect those who draw near. . . . But when Christ had offered for all time a single sacrifice for sins, he sat down at the right hand of God, then to wait until his enemies should be made a stool for his feet. For by a single offering, he has perfected for all time those who are sanctified" (Heb. 10:1, 12–14). In Hebrews, the argument is not against Jews as such, even though Judaism is considered outmoded because the author understands it to be an imperfect religious system now brought to completion by the perfect sacrifice of Jesus. Unlike John, however, the writer to the Hebrews refrains from making final, negative judgments about the fate of Jews who do not believe in Jesus. Old Testament heroes and heroines are said to have possessed authentic faith in God (ch. 11), and one cryptic passage implies that this faith finally apprehends its object through the sanctification of Christians (see 11:39–40). In some vicarious manner Christian faith functions *on behalf of* Jews.

The writer of 1 Pet. 2:5–10 claims for Christian believers many of the titles which the Hebrew Scriptures assign to Jews as a whole (chosen race, royal priesthood, holy nation, people of God); but significantly, the Petrine author does not use a definite article with any of these titles, which means that he never denies their ongoing validity for unbelieving Jews. Concerning the latter, he states simply: "They stumble because they disobey the word, as they were destined to do" (1 Pet. 2:8). Paul says this same thing in Rom. 10:18–11:10, 30f., but he resists the further conclusion that unbelieving Jews are destined to stumble "so as to fall," i.e., be lost forever (Rom. 11:11ff.). We have insufficient grounds for reading into 1 Pet. 2:5–10 a developed "replacement" theology like John's whereby the church supersedes empirical Israel as God's chosen nation.

Two passages in Revelation (2:9; 3:9) suggest that the Christian readers addressed may be Jews troubled by "those who say that they are Jews and are not, but are a synagogue of Satan." Perhaps the author refers here to all Jews who reject Jesus' Messiahship, but it is equally possible that he has in mind only particular groups of Jews, and perhaps even those Christian Jews whom he regards as heretics. One finds no developed polemic in Revelation against Jews or Judaism as such.

Chapter 7
ISRAEL AT THE HEART OF THE CHURCH

1. Again, John represents the chief exception to this general rule. He seems to retain a hope for the general resurrection and final judgment "sometime" (Jn. 5:28f.; 12:48), but he shows more interest in eternal life here and now.

2. Contrast a statement made by Rabbi Jakob Petuchowski to the Third National Workshop on Jewish-Christian Relations (1977): "God has the final answers [to Jewish-Christian dialogue]—they will surprise us." Reported by Charles Angell, S.A., "New Candor in the Jewish-Christian Dialogue," *Ecumenical Trends*, Vol. 6, No. 9 (Oct. 1977), p. 134.

3. I am positively inclined toward Ruether's argument in support of an unfulfilled messianism for Christians based on God's single, once-for-all covenant with Israel. See *Faith and Fratricide*, pp. 246–257. To Ruether's thoughts I would add only two observations: *(a)* the proleptic dimension of Christology which she advocates is nothing new since it was central to the thinking of most New Testament authors; *(b)* they, however, balanced it with a joyful sense of the Spirit's activity.

4. It is beyond the scope of our study to evaluate that movement in some Jewish and Christian circles which is coming to be known as Holocaust theology. For an overview, see Fleischner, *Auschwitz: Beginning of a New Era? Reflections on the Holocaust.* In my view, there are good grounds for seeing the Holocaust as a divine challenge to traditional Christian understandings of salvation history, especially those which presume a progressive, triumphal march of God's grace via the church to all humankind.

5. See Sandmel, *Anti-Semitism in the New Testament?* pp. 162–164.

6. See the Selected Bibliography.

7. An example would be the passion narrative compiled by John T. Townsend, cited in Sandmel, *Anti-Semitism in the New Testament?* p. 163. See also Eugene Fisher, *Faith Without Prejudice* (Paulist Press, 1977), pp. 98–118.

8. Luke's Magnificat (Lk. 1:46–55) and Nunc Dimittis (Lk. 2:29–32) have found their way into the liturgies of many Christian churches. Both of these hymns use the word "Israel" to designate the Jewish people. This comes through with special clarity in Lk. 2:32, where Simeon foresees in the baby Jesus "a light for revelation to the Gentiles, and for glory to thy people Israel." The standard eucharistic prayer in the new *Lutheran Book of Worship* also takes care to speak of "Israel, your chosen people," without refer-

ring to the church. See *Lutheran Book of Worship* (Augsburg Publishing House and Fortress Press, 1978), pp. 69, 89, 110.

9. A helpful case study on this subject is "The Gospel Sources of Christian-Jewish Prejudice: Teaching Church School Teachers to Apply Contemporary Biblical Studies to the Task of Interpreting the Problematic Gospel Texts" by David C. Kaminsky. Unpublished D.Min. thesis-project, Princeton Theological Seminary, 1976.

10. Many good suggestions for initiating local dialogues can be found in Paul J. Kirsch's *We Christians and Jews* (Fortress Press, 1975), pp. 122–141. For reports on regional, national, and international discussions, two newsletters stand out: *Ecumenical Trends*, published by the Graymoor Ecumenical Institute (Roman Catholic) of Garrison, New York; and *Face to Face*, published by the Anti-Defamation League of B'nai B'rith in New York City (with an editorial board comprised of Jews and Christians).

11. Especially among scholars, however, more contemporary Jews than ever before are taking an interest in the New Testament documents. Some of the prominent names here are David Flusser and Pinchas Lapide in Israel; Hans-Joachim Schoeps in Germany; Jacob Neusner and Samuel Sandmel in the United States. Enlightening on this score is a published discussion between Hans Küng and Dr. Lapide, during which the latter refers to twenty-nine recent books in Hebrew on Jesus. See "Is Jesus a Bond or Barrier? A Jewish-Christian Dialogue," *Journal of Ecumenical Studies*, Vol. 14, No. 3 (Summer 1977), pp. 466–483, esp. p. 471.

12. See Charles Angell's "New Candor in the Jewish-Christian Dialogue," referred to in note 2, above.

13. The phrase is Krister Stendahl's and occurs in his *Paul Among Jews and Gentiles*, p. 37.

14. In referring to Israel's permanent status as God's elect people, Paul notes that "the gifts and the call of God are irrevocable" (Rom. 11:29). The Greek word for "gifts" in this passage is *charismata* (sg. *charisma*), an expression which the apostle elsewhere reserves for gifts of the Spirit distinctive to Christians (e.g., 1 Cor. 1:7; 7:7; chs. 12–14; Rom. 12:1–8). By employing this loaded word, Paul reminds his Gentile readers that Israel stands with them (and before them!) as a people uniquely blessed with concrete manifestations of God's grace (see Rom. 9:4–5).

SELECTED BIBLIOGRAPHY

Alon, G. *Jews, Judaism, and the Classical World.* Tr. by I. Abrahams. Jerusalem: The Magnes Press, Hebrew University, 1977.

Bammel, Ernst, ed. *The Trial of Jesus: Cambridge Studies in Honour of C. F. D. Moule.* London: SCM Press, 1970.

Barth, Markus. *Jesus the Jew.* Tr. by F. Prussner. John Knox Press, 1978.

Bowker, John. *Jesus and the Pharisees.* Cambridge University Press, 1973.

Brown, Raymond E. *The Gospel According to John.* 2 vols. The Anchor Bible. Doubleday & Co., 1966, 1970.

Cook, M. J. *Mark's Treatment of the Jewish Leaders.* Leiden: E. J. Brill, 1978.

Davies, William David. *The Gospel and the Land: Early Christianity and Jewish Territorial Doctrine.* University of California Press, 1974.

————. "Paul and the People of Israel," *New Testament Studies,* Vol. 24 (1977), pp. 4–39.

————. *Paul and Rabbinic Judaism.* London: S.P.C.K., 1962.

————. *The Setting of the Sermon on the Mount.* Cambridge University Press, 1964.

Epp, E. J. "Anti-Semitism and the Popularity of the Fourth Gos-

175

pel," *Central Conference of American Rabbis Journal,* Vol. 22 (1975), pp. 35–57.

Fisher, Eugene. *Faith Without Prejudice: Rebuilding Christian Attitudes Toward Judaism.* Paulist Press, 1977.

Fleischner, Eva, ed. *Auschwitz: Beginning of a New Era? Reflections on the Holocaust.* Anti-Defamation League of B'nai B'rith, KTAV Publishing House, 1977.

Flusser, David. *Jesus.* Tr. by Ronald Walls. Herder & Herder, 1969.

Grant, Michael. *The Jews in the Roman World.* Charles Scribner's Sons, 1973.

Hamerton-Kelly, R., and Scroggs, R., eds. *Jews, Greeks, and Christians. Religious Cultures in Late Antiquity: Essays in Honor of William David Davies.* Leiden: E. J. Brill, 1976.

Hengel, Martin. *Judaism and Hellenism: Studies in Their Encounter in Palestine During the Early Hellenistic Period.* 2 vols. Tr. by John Bowden. Fortress Press, 1974.

Herford, R. Travers. *Christianity in Talmud and Midrash.* Reference Book Publishers, 1966.

———. *Pirke Aboth: The Ethics of the Talmud. The Sayings of the Fathers.* Tr. and commentary by R. Travers Herford. Schocken Books, 1962.

Heschel, Abraham J. *Israel: An Echo of Eternity.* Farrar, Straus & Giroux, 1971.

Jeremias, Joachim. *Jerusalem in the Time of Jesus: An Investigation Into Economic and Social Conditions During the New Testament Period.* Tr. by F. H. and C. H. Cave. Fortress Press, 1969.

Jervell, Jacob. *Luke and the People of God: A New Look at Luke-Acts.* Augsburg Publishing House, 1972.

Jervell, Jacob, and Meeks, Wayne A., eds. *God's Christ and His People: Studies in Honour of Nils Alstrup Dahl.* Oslo: Universitetsforlaget, 1978.

Kirsch, Paul J. *We Christians and Jews.* Fortress Press, 1975.

Lapide, Pinchas. *Israelis, Jews, and Jesus.* Foreword by Samuel Sandmel. Tr. by Peter Heinegg. Doubleday & Co., 1979.

Martyn, James Louis. *The Gospel of John in Christian History: Essays for Interpreters.* Paulist Press, 1979.

————. *History and Theology in the Fourth Gospel.* Harper & Row, Publishers, 1968; rev. and enl. ed., Abingdon Press, 1979.

Meeks, Wayne A., and Wilken, Robert L. *Jews and Christians in Antioch in the First Four Centuries of the Common Era.* Scholars Press, 1978.

Neusner, Jacob. *Early Rabbinic Judaism: Historical Studies in Religion, Literature and Art.* Leiden: E. J. Brill, 1975.

————. *From Politics to Piety: The Emergence of Pharisaic Judaism.* Prentice-Hall, 1973.

————. *The Rabbinic Traditions About the Pharisees Before 70.* Leiden: E. J. Brill, 1970.

Parkes, James W. *The Conflict of the Church and the Synagogue: A Study in the Origins of Antisemitism.* Jewish Publication Society of America, 1961.

Rubenstein, Richard L. *My Brother Paul.* Harper & Row, Publishers, 1972.

Ruether, Rosemary. *Faith and Fratricide: The Theological Roots of Anti-Semitism.* Seabury Press, 1974.

Safrai, S., and Stern, M., in cooperation with D. Flusser and W. C. van Unnik. *The Jewish People in the First Century: Historical Geography, Political History, Social, Cultural and Religious Life and Institutions.* Assen: Van Gorcum, 1974.

Sanders, Ed Parish. *Paul and Palestinian Judaism: A Comparison of Patterns of Religion.* Fortress Press, 1977.

Sandmel, Samuel. *Anti-Semitism in the New Testament?* Fortress Press, 1978.

Schechter, Solomon. *Aspects of Rabbinic Theology: Major Concepts of the Talmud.* Schocken Books, 1961.

Schoeps, Hans-Joachim. *Jewish Christianity: Factional Disputes in the Early Church.* Tr. by D. R. A. Hare. Fortress Press, 1969.

————. *Paul: The Theology of the Apostle in the Light of Jewish Religious History.* Tr. by Harold Knight. Westminster Press, 1961.

Scholem, Gershom G. *Major Trends in Jewish Mysticism.* Schocken Books, 1967.

————. *The Messianic Idea in Judaism and Other Essays on Jewish Spirituality.* Schocken Books, 1972.

Schürer, Emil. *The History of the Jewish People in the Age of Jesus Christ* (175 B.C.–A.D.135). A new English version, rev. and ed. by Géza Vermès and Fergus Millar. Edinburgh: T. & T. Clark, 1973.

Simon, Marcel. *Jewish Sects at the Time of Jesus.* Tr. by James H. Farley. Fortress Press, 1967.

Sloyan, Gerard S. *Is Christ the End of the Law?* Westminster Press, 1978.

————. *Jesus on Trial: The Development of the Passion Narratives and Their Historical and Ecumenical Implications.* Fortress Press, 1973.

Stendahl, Krister. *Paul Among Jews and Gentiles.* Fortress Press, 1976.

Theissen, Gerd. *Sociology of Early Palestinian Christianity.* Tr. by John Bowden. Fortress Press, 1978.

Vermès, Géza. *Jesus the Jew.* Macmillan Publishing Co., 1973.

Wilson, William Riley. *The Execution of Jesus: A Judicial, Literary, and Historical Investigation.* Charles Scribner's Sons, 1970.

Winter, Paul. *On the Trial of Jesus.* Berlin: Töpelmann Verlag, 1961.

INDEX OF BIBLICAL REFERENCES